# Emerging From Chaos

## Addressing the Emotions of the Pandemic

Alan Cutter

Edited by Ann Cutter

Emerging from Chaos

Copyright © 2020 Alan Cutter

All rights reserved.

ISBN: 979-8-6524-3542-4

# DEDICATION

*For Isaac, Asa, Sasha and Theo, my grandchildren*

*You are the change that is needed.*

*Your lives matter!*

Emerging from Chaos

# Table of Contents

| | |
|---|---|
| Preface | 7 |
| The Back Story | 9 |
| Discussion Suggestions | 29 |
| The Gift You Bring | 36 |
| Coping with Crisis | 39 |
| Setting the Stage | 55 |
| The Alphabet Begins | 59 |

Anger, Boredom, Concerned, Depressed, Exhausted, Fear, Guilty, Helpless, Isolated, Jealous, Knowing, Labeled, Manipulated, Nervous, Overwhelmed, Presence, Queasy, Restless, Sadness, Tempted, Unknown, Vulnerable, Wistful, Xenophobia, Yearning, Zen

| | |
|---|---|
| Final Thoughts | 111 |
| About the Author | 115 |

Scripture Passages

Scripture quotations marked NRSV are from the New Revised Standard Version of the Bible, copyright © 1989 by the Division of Christian Education of the National Council of the Churches of Christ in the United States of America. Used by permission. All rights reserved.

Scripture Quotations marked ESV are from the Holy Bible, English Standard Version, copyright © 2001 by Crossway Bibles, a publishing ministry of Good News Publishers. Used by permission. All rights reserved.

"Sunrise at Gulfport"
Cover Photograph © Ann Cutter

Author Photograph © Anna Garnett

The videos associated with this book are available on YouTube under the title "Emerging From Chaos." There is no charge to use them.

# PREFACE

Alan is a retired Presbyterian pastor. He is also a Vietnam veteran, a disabled veteran, living with post-traumatic stress disorder (PTSD) and Agent Orange related Parkinson's disease.

The PTSD came first. With the help of counselors at VET Centers and companions in a veterans' organization, and with the support of a wonderful and compassionate congregation in Duluth, Minnesota, Alan confronted that diagnosis and determinedly claimed his life, recognizing that PTSD and the trauma of war would always be a part of who he was.

In 2010, Veterans Administration doctors diagnosed Alan with Parkinson's disease. In one of those coincidences that astound us his diagnosis came in the same month that Parkinson's disease was declared an Agent Orange "presumptive," that is to say, if one had "boots on the ground" and develops Parkinson's disease, it is assumed that Agent Orange is the cause and no further substantiation is required.

Alan had been able to work while living with PTSD, but the combination of Parkinson's disease and PTSD made it impossible for him to continue.

He retired a bit earlier than he had planned. The combination of the PTSD and the Parkinson's affects his ability to concentrate; it takes him a long time to complete tasks that he used to do rather quickly.

I hasten to add that his sense of humor and the ridiculous remains strong and his ability to make outrageous puns is as maddening as ever. His intellect and faith have not been shaken. He is not depressed about the Parkinson's disease; as he says, he went through all of that "emotional shit" with the initial diagnosis of PTSD and does not need to do it again, even if people think he should! We enjoy our children and grandchildren, traveling here and there to see old friends and make new ones, and helping others, as we are able. Physically, Alan will tell people that he is slower moving and a little unsteady; he says he has one-cane days, two-cane days, and occasionally no-cane days.

In late 2017, we moved into a Continuing Care Retirement Community so we would no longer have to worry about a piece of property but could be free to travel and spend time with family. Then this pandemic hit, and we find ourselves in an unexpected situation!

However, that journey is by no means over and we consistently enjoy new adventures and insights. We hope that the thoughts and stories and concepts contained in this book will help others in their journeys of healing.

Ann (and Alan) Cutter

St Petersburg, FL

2020

# The Back Story

IN THE BEGINNING there were stories, often confusing, almost contradictory versions. So it is in my faith tradition, Judeo-Christian, with the two stories of creation found in *Genesis*. And the confusion of voices does not stop there, but continues into the New Testament with the "Four Gospels," each presenting a different conception of Jesus and his ministry. All of this forms the "back story" for my understanding when I speak of my own faith.

So, here is the story told through the following Facebook posts that form a major part of the "back story" of this video series and book. These are particular "back stories" from my faith journey, sometimes confusing, sometimes contradictory.

When the COVID-19 crisis began we, at our Continuing Care Retirement Community (CCRC), were in the middle of Lent with Holy Week almost upon us. As the dire warnings began to cause panic and fear, we were fortunate that our community, already in place, was able to act with concern and compassion by locking down both the Health Center and assisted living facility. Our own community chaplain was in a fourteen-day quarantine period having been exposed to the virus and therefore was not able to be present on campus. I was concerned that, because of the sudden onset of the lock-down and the imminent start of what many had experienced as a major faith holiday, Easter, there would be great confusion if nothing was being said. So I decided to write brief meditations to be shared daily with those in the assisted living facility as well as, if they wished, with the residents in independent living. This is what I could do.

So I started writing brief thoughts that could help people find a focus for Holy Week. I decided to concentrate on the concept of "helpers." It was not going to be much, but the reflections shared would at least be a presence. And on my own Facebook page, I started to reflect on what I was doing and why. This is where the "back story" to this video series and book begins.

<u>Posted Friday, April 3, 2020</u>

As a church pastor I worked with a set calendar that included a fiscal year, a school year, and a liturgical year, among others. The big churchy holidays revolved around Christmas and Easter. Let me just think about Easter – preparations would have been underway for several months – choir rehearsals, Lenten programming, ordering the palms for Palm Sunday and lilies and other flowers for Easter Sunday, and so on, all the while maintaining the rhythm of the regular ongoing work of the church. Even when I was in South Louisiana following Katrina/Rita, and then Gustav/Ike, we still managed to use the holidays as focal and rallying points. But this year . . . it is different. No sunrise services, no Easter breakfasts, no watering of the flowers trying to keep them fresh, none of that. Oh, we have the wonders of electronic and digital communication on a variety of platforms, and everyone is struggling to get up to speed. Yet there is none of the travel to family gatherings, buying of Easter finery, planning of large meals, and so on. Other religious traditions are facing similar disruptions. My wife and I are encouraged – strongly – not to leave our community, but to stay at home, the two of us being considered a "germ sharing unit." Over my life, the Christian holidays have always been a part of the year, Easter especially as it is the foundation of my faith community. But there was one year I lost Easter, did not know when it was being celebrated, never really even thought about it; Easter was just not there. I was in Vietnam. It was not until years later, literally years later, that I realized that in 1972 I had missed Easter. Being curious, I looked up the dates of Easter of 1972 and, by consulting histories of the Vietnam War, THEN I knew where I was around Easter of 1972. The consuming event of that time in Vietnam is known as the Easter Invasion. When I learned that, I knew exactly what I was doing on the days around Easter. And what I was doing had nothing to do with empty tombs and lilies, alleluias and family gatherings.

## Posted Saturday, April 4, 2020

In a post yesterday I wrote about the Easter I lost while I was in Vietnam, discovering later – much later – that the period of Easter in 1972 coincided with what became known as the Easter Invasion. Having this information, I realized I had pretty vivid memories of that period of time. When the whole business started I was the lone American standing watch in the Vietnamese Naval Coastal Surveillance Center in Danang. Over the radios I heard the opening shots [at a Vietnamese Navy Unit near the Demilitarized Zone {DMZ}] and the increasingly panic-stricken calls for help until the radios went silent. No one answered our calls. In many ways, the situation deteriorated quickly after that initial burst – much like the current COVID19 Crisis. However, I do not want to stop my narrative with the closing words of the previous post: "what I was doing had nothing to do with empty tombs and lilies, alleluias and family gatherings." A good friend and Vietnam veteran replied to that post telling me about his "missing Vietnam Easter," a time he labeled as "a disaster." I wrote back to him because for me that missing Easter was a complex mix of activities and emotions. I had neither the time to evaluate those activities nor an opportunity to experience the emotions; I simply "did what had to be done" and moved on. However, later – much later – I did that hard work. The result, as I expressed it to my friend, was this: "As I have looked back at that experience, over those few days, I have discovered that in my actions there was a semblance of integrity and a graceful gift that both helped me survive and gave me hope." Forgive me if I do not get more specific; war leaves both harsh and tender memories. What I want to emphasize is that even in the worst of events, when I reviewed my activities, I found I could say that I did my best to support the mission I had been assigned as well as my best to fulfill the oath I had taken as a United States Naval officer. In addition, during all that was happening, the value of my life was affirmed in a way that sustained me through the horrors that were still to occur. I write this not to boast of my good fortune, but because I want to bear witness to the reality that even in the worst of times there occur small acts, often unnoticed or appreciated, small acts of caring and compassion that are easily overlooked and too often forgotten under the overwhelming horror of an event. I want to encourage each of us, during this distressing time, not to be so involved that we cannot see the many small ways that life is affirmed around us, for if we miss these seemingly insignificant moments, and the people involved, then we will never understand the story of Holy Week. With this background in my mind and soul, I wrote the first of my short thoughts for Palm Sunday through Easter, brief words that are being shared with our residents in Assisted Living and independent living:

### *A Holy Week Practice – Looking for the Helpers*
### *Palm Sunday, April 5, 2020*

*Presbyterian minster Fred Rodgers, best known as "Mr. Rodgers" often told this story about when he was a boy and would see scary things on the news: "My mother would say to me, "Always look for the helpers. There's always someone who is trying to help." I did, and I came to see that the world is full of doctors and nurses, police and firemen, volunteers, neighbors and friends who are ready to jump in to help when things go wrong."*

*During this frightening time, we need to look for the helpers! Beginning today, Palm Sunday, and daily now thru Easter, a short note will challenge you to look for the helpers in our lives and to give thanks for them.*

*Today we remember how Jesus entered Jerusalem riding upon the back of a donkey. The people greeted him with shouts of "Hosanna!" and spread on the road branches cut from the trees. Who were the helpers who cut and gathered the branches for the crowd to throw so that Jesus' path might be less dusty, softer underfoot for the animal upon which he was riding? Who has helped smooth your path during the scary times of life?*

<u>Posted Sunday, April 5, 2020</u>

Part of what I am trying to convey in these daily Holy Week meditations is that important helpers are around us in our everyday lives; often unnoticed, their small acts have a great influence on our lives. A few kind words can make a huge difference. While I was in Vietnam I received a "call" to the ministry. This was definitely not part of my life plan! So I was greatly surprised when, in the midst of a tense encounter with a superior officer, I publically declared my intention to go to seminary. In that moment I literally threw away my own dream of what I would do in life to say that I was going to do that one thing I had vowed I never would – go into my father's business, so to speak. My tour of duty in Vietnam was difficult and lonely. My parents sensed my frustration, anger, and pain. My father had shared their concerns with Graham, a church friend who had been a Navy officer in WW2, the executive officer on the first LST to arrive on Omaha Beach with needed supplies. When I returned from Vietnam, I accompanied my parents to a service at the church they attended when vacationing in southern Maine. During the service I felt so disconnected and lonely I almost fled from the sanctuary. When I came out of the church, anxious to escape, Graham and his wife Jean were waiting. Jean deftly inserted herself between my parents, while Graham, firmly grasping my arm, led me out under the large tree that then stood in front of the church. As we looked out over the cemetery towards the water, Graham told me that my father had spoken to him about me. Doing his duty at Omaha Beach, he said, had left him deeply troubled. "I watched you in church. I could see you squirming. I know that discomfort. You carry, as do I, the unspeakable burden of having witnessed the evil of war. It will be painful, but you will have to sort that out. But I want to give you a new assignment, a new duty, one that will be more difficult then you can imagine. " Graham, holding my arm captive, turned me so he could look right at me, and continued, "I want you to be a witness to the reality of hope. Even though you have seen the worst side of humanity, I want you to live a life seeing and encouraging the good, the sacred, in each person. Now here is the real challenge: to live that life you have to see the good in yourself. I can't tell you how to do that; I found my way through love. Your task is finding your own way, but start that journey now. It is worth it. I did it; and I believe you can do it too. I see it in you." We looked in silence at each other. I considered the last five words, and simply said, "Thank you." Then we went and got some lemonade. My parents were curious and asked me what Graham said. I told them he spoke briefly of his experience and was glad to see I had survived. I did not go any further then that. I had not told them of the "call" I had received; what I had been doing did not seem to be a suitable preparation for a religious occupation. I was mightily confused, doubting that God really meant it. However, Graham's last five words echoed the call I had received. That afternoon, in a rocking chair on the front porch of our house, as I started to sort things out, I made a decision to answer the call. To myself I said, "If God and Graham see some possibility, some good, in me, then I'll risk it." In truth, I had more faith in Graham's judgment then I did in God's, perhaps because Graham was right there and God seemed so far away.

## *A Holy Week Practice – Looking for the Helpers*
## *Monday of Holy Week, April 6, 2020*

*After Jesus entered Jerusalem he spent much of his time teaching; his method was to tell stories he called "parables." One was about a wedding feast given by a king to which none of the guests came! The king, wanting the feast to be a celebration, sent his servants into the streets to invite everyone to the banquet. Who are the helpers that invite us into that banquet we call life?*

Posted Tuesday, April 7, 2020

The helpers in life are often hidden, not even recognized at the time. Only much later in life is their serendipitous influence acknowledged. For me, music has always been a powerful influence. Just like the old chiefs at Boot Camp, at least they all seemed old to us as young recruits, I now choke up when I hear the opening notes of the Navy Hymn; by the time I get through the opening phrase, "Eternal Father strong to save, whose arm hath bound the restless wave," my eyes are clouded by tears. (As recruits singing in the Blue

Jacket Choir, we sometimes used the sentimentality of the chiefs to our advantage, but that's another story.) I have written about how, after I returned from Vietnam, I felt like an alien in my homeland. Songs with phrases like "I want to go home . . ." would pop up on the radio while I was driving and I would pull off the road sobbing. (*Sloop John B*) Hearing the phrase "Don't you know me, I'm your native son . . ." would arouse such strong, conflicting emotions that I would have to go somewhere alone to try and sort out the feelings. (*City of New Orleans*) Words of the hymns sung in church would often ambush me, making my task as pastor difficult. By the time I arrived in Duluth, MN, to begin my pastorate there, I was growing increasingly desperate to find some way to suppress these debilitating emotions. Serendipity again interfered in my life for the interim pastor preceding me had left a packet of information about helping agencies in the area, one of which was a VET Center. It was with great trepidation that just before Easter of 1991, with two funerals just before Easter and two just after, all of them veterans and three of them Navy veterans, that I staggered into the building housing that office and said I was a Vietnam Veteran and I had a problem. A counselor came out to speak with me briefly; she had no free time at that moment, but would I like to make an appointment? I demurred and said I would simply come back and prepared to escape. However, the counselor insisted I make an appointment and the day after Easter I, very reluctantly, sat down in a VET Center chair and started cautiously, very cautiously, to talk. I wanted a Band-Aid to put over my wound; instead, thanks to the relentless push of the hidden helpers in music, this was the first step in my long walk home.

## *A Holy Week Practice - Looking for the Helpers Tuesday of Holy Week, April 7, 2020*

*After Jesus entered Jerusalem he answered many questions that were asked to trap him. One question was "Which commandment is the greatest?" Jesus replied, "You shall love the Lord your God with all your heart, and all your soul, and all your mind. This is the greatest and first commandment. And a second is like it: You shall love your neighbor as yourself." Who helped you to love your neighbors? How?*

<u>Posted Wednesday, April 8, 2020</u>

Throughout our lives, we human beings seem to expect events will happen in particular places. If I were to ask you, where would you go to look for helpers, you might well suggest I journey to a soup kitchen, or to a work camp at a recent disaster, or to go to the local fire station or emergency room. Undoubtedly there would be a wide range of suggestions based on our assumptions about where one could find people helping other people. However, helpers do show up at unexpected times in unexpected places, and often those helpers do not realize how they are helping another person! In 1991 I was at a meeting of veterans who were all clergy; I had gone to that meeting hoping to find some relief from the internal anguish I felt concerning events in Vietnam. I had listened to the presentations, but had not participated in the discussions. We had a free night; all but two attending the conference had gone to visit a local AMVETS chapter, knowing that the veterans there would be happy to buy drinks for the "chaplains." I was one of the two who stayed back; joining me was an Episcopalian priest, a former Marine officer who, a few weeks into his tour of duty, had lost his legs when he triggered a land mine. His name coincidentally was also Alan. Being the only two at the retreat center we fell into conversation; Alan had a fifth of Scotch and I had a fifth of Bourbon. By the time the rest of the company rolled in, we had pretty much polished off our bottles. However, a Catholic priest, the convener of this gathering, sat down with us for a nightcap. Alan and I each contributed some of our fifths to his glass. As we "stood up" to stagger off to bed the priest insisted we share a prayer together; so we did. I do not remember the prayer offered in that circle of inebriated clergy, but I do recall the words just prior to the prayer: "Remember, the only thing we really have to share with each other is our stories." That changed my life. Unfortunately my friend Alan, though he remained a member of our group, never really was able to complete the healing journey, and years later, at the beginning of another American conflict when a number of Marines had been killed, he committed suicide. It fell to me to notify the rest of the group; it felt very strange, all things considered, to send out a message that started, "Today Alan killed himself." That Fall when our group gathered once again and held our own memorial service for Alan, his wife Betsy came to join us and stayed with us for the week of the conference. As was our custom, even though we came from a wide variety of traditions, we set aside any denominational or doctrinal issues so that we might celebrate the Lord's Supper, Communion, a Eucharist together. Part of the liturgy we used involved "passing the peace," a process we did very intentionally so that each person greeted all the others. When I came round the circle to Betsy, I hugged her and "Peace be with you, Betsy," and she said "Peace be with you, Alan." Immediately she, still in the embrace we shared, froze; after a few seconds she said, "I never expected to say that again!" While the circle of sharing continued around us, we cried together. Betsy came to our yearly meetings after that, until cancer took her from us, saying that our group was an important part of her own healing journey. Helpers come at unexpected times in unexpected ways. Look for them and give thanks.

### *A Holy Week Practice – Looking for the Helpers*
### *Wednesday of Holy Week, April 8, 2020*

*After Jesus entered Jerusalem he spent time with his disciples instructing them by word and example. He even poured water into a basin and washed the disciples' feet, saying, "If I have washed your feet, you also ought to wash one another's feet. For I have set an example, that you should also do as I have done to you." Who are the helpers that have washed your hands and feet?*

Posted Thursday, April 9, 2020, Maundy Thursday

Water. A pitcher. A basin. A towel. Helpers often use simple things to carry out tasks. Today is Maundy Thursday, the day we remember how Jesus used water, a pitcher, a basin, a towel to wash the disciples feet. Water, a pitcher, a basin, a towel were the helping items I used when baptizing a child or an adult. Bread is taken, blessed, broken, shared; wine is taken, blessed, poured out, shared;

these are the helping elements used when recalling how Jesus ate his final meal with the disciples. For me, Maundy Thursday is hard day. Simple things have a profound effect on me for simple things matter greatly, having played such an important part in my life's journey, reminding me of both the blessings and the curses of life. Let me tell you a story from my life. I was at Austin Seminary at a Continuing Education event during Lent; it was mid-March; there was a chapel service and I went expecting a normal Seminary service – rather dry and stuffy. Here is what I wrote that evening.

*Well, it happened again. You'd think I learn but apparently I haven't, or I'd forgotten, or I let my guard down, one or the other, something like that. I got ambushed in a seminary chapel – again. Walking into the stone cruciform from the side, sliding across a pew, finding a seat, getting a program – everything was fine. Then I looked up to the front of the church. There was a blue and white ceramic washbasin with a large, matching pitcher next to it. I saw them and I was transported back, back to L-----'s kitchen and the day the barriers, our personal perimeters, came down. Just the sight of these items summoned an image long buried, and then other things flooded into me – the smell of bread and fish, the bitter taste of the scotch I was drinking, even the sound of the water boiling in the huge pot on the stove, waiting to be poured into the basin where L------ was trying to get my clothes clean, washing away the blood of the previous night's killings. And with all of this, other memories came as well – fast and furious. Wandering helplessly in and out of awareness, I gripped my cane tightly in my hands; I glanced around the chapel, wondering if I could cut and run. I couldn't. I'd have to sit and gut it out – again – and hope that I wasn't making a scene, sweating, shivering, tears flowing. Worship with me as a participant is always a risk. That's one reason I like to be in charge. I can often, though not always, reduce the risk of an ambush. "Lord, draw near; draw near and stay" went the song. I frankly wanted no one near; I wanted to be alone. "O Son of God, source of life," I was remembering death, death, and how far I had been from life and how I drew close to life with L------. Then another song "Let the fires of your justice burn!" Justice? The wildfires I knew were far from any "fires of justice." Justice, fairness, concepts that didn't enter into my life in Vietnam, or even, I fear, in my relationship with L------. I had the power—all of it, or so I thought. The attack subsided as the prayers were offered. The service ended. We were invited to come to the "font" and touch the water and anoint ourselves. Some did; others didn't. I did not want to; I really wanted to. So I did it. I went forward, dipped my hand in the water, touched my forehead, my face, trying to do what I had seen L------ doing – wash the blood away.*

## A Holy Week Practice – Looking for the Helpers
## Thursday of Holy Week, April 9, 2020

*As the Passover began, Jesus ate a final meal with his disciples. During the course of that meal, it is recorded by John that Jesus said, "This is my commandment, that you love one another as I have loved you. No one has greater love than this, to lay down one's life for one's friends." Often those who rush to help others do so at the risk of their own lives. Today, who are these helpers? Pray for them and their families.*

### Posted Friday, April 10, 2020, Good Friday

Each of us may have own image of God; I know I do. My image is neither George Burns nor Morgan Freeman, who have both played that exalted role, but is shaped by something I saw on television in the mid-1950s. My father was then the pastor of a Congregational Church in North Leominster, MA. We lived in an extremely small, supposedly efficient, ranch house parsonage, and we had a black and white television. The Asian flu was the epidemic that year, and I had been very, very sick, missing weeks of school. Television was still fairly new to society so no one worried about children watching too much. For my parents it was a Godsend; it was something I could do when I was able to sit up, but still too weak to move. I remember being plopped, half awake, in front of the TV and just watching whatever came on. One day what was shown was "The

Green Pastures," a movie presenting Biblical stories with all the characters portrayed by African-Americans, and heaven was an eternal "fish fry." I was fascinated by the movie and by the filler that followed: a program featuring the black singer Marian Anderson in concert. The result in my muddled mind was that the image of God I saw, and still have, is a large black woman who sings, a combination of Marian Anderson and Aunt Jemima. Perhaps you have an image of Jesus based upon the popular pictures of the longhaired, handsome white men who seemed to populate both the King James and the Revised Standard versions of the Bible. Even Jesus on the cross giving up his life for others was a pretty heroic portrayal of a good looking white guy. I have my own image of the face of Jesus. I was doing something I was not supposed to do, flying as a passenger on a helicopter with a Vietnamese crew. We were shot down and landed hard in the middle of a firefight so we became a good target. I happened to have with me a small radio, a battery-operated PRC25, and I went up on the guard channel to call for help, not expecting much. The machine was on fire behind me and the situation was definitely going down hill fast; I was concentrating on finding targets when the Vietnamese beside me, who looked like a teen-ager, hit me in the back of the head, and pointed over to the left, gave me a shove, and yelled "Go!" An American helicopter was coming in fast with a jungle penetrator (a rescue device) hanging down; the door gunner was lighting up the tree line. I went, emptying my clip at the tree line, and caught the penetrator, put down the flaps, hopped on, and the pilot took off with me flopping around down below, bouncing off a tree and slowly being winched up into the ship. I was semi-conscious at best, but they dropped me off with a Vietnamese army unit who got me to the Vietnamese Rehab Hospital in Danang. There I was given a cane to help me walk; I hitched a ride back to my duty station in time to take the night watch with the Vietnamese at the Command Center. When I think of Jesus giving up his life for me I see the grim face of a young Vietnamese man facing death looking at me yelling, "Go! Go!" And I am full of conflicting emotions, but one is supreme: I am grateful.

## *A Holy Week Practice – Looking for the Helpers*
## *Good Friday, April 10, 2020*

*It is hard to think of helpers on Good Friday when so many were focused on killing the troublemaker Jesus. But they were there at the Cross – witnesses whose presence, words, and actions contribute to the story – his mother Mary, and Mary the mother of James and Joseph, and Mary Magdalene as well as the apostle John; the truth-telling centurion who said, "Certainly this man was innocent;" and Joseph of Arimathea who took the body and placed it in a tomb. All were helpers on this day, for the greatest gift we share is the gift of telling the story of faith. Who do you count among the helpers in your life and on this day? Who told you the story of faith?*

<u>Posted Saturday, April 11, 2020</u>

Holy Week has its own terror for pastors. Beginning with Ash Wednesday and moving forward with the special programming for whatever the Lenten focus might be in any particular year plus getting ready for the labors of Holy Week is exhausting! Where's the wooden cross for the Sanctuary? Are the purple paraments clean? Do we have enough candles for Tenebrae? Is the music set? Have the palms been ordered? What about the Easter breakfast? Are there enough lilies and other flowers? Who is in charge of watering them until they can be set in place on the Saturday before Easter? Who is in charge of the distribution of the flowers? The list goes on and on and on. How many special services are there going to be during the week? What about music for the early service? And now this year, all the Lent and Holy Week plans have been thrown into disarray! Personally, I would be glad of one thing; I could avoid the dreaded Easter lilies! They are messy, demanding, and the odor is too sweet. They make me sneeze and my nose has run constantly every Easter Sunday. I do, however, have my own flower that carries for me the Easter message of hope. In 1992, I attended a conference in California. Outside my room at the retreat center was a small flower garden, and I enjoyed in the morning, throughout the day, and in the evening, simply going out and sitting on the garden bench. When I first arrived I had noticed a number of rose bushes, some still having a few remaining buds. There was one bush that had a bud just ready to burst, and every time I went and sat in the garden, something I did quite often, I would check to see if that bud had opened. As the week progressed it looked each morning as if this would be the day, but by evening it was still closed tight. By mid-week I was getting quite impatient with that plant. The week had not gone as I had planned, and this stubborn bud was not helping. Then on the last day of the conference, things changed for me. By the grace of God, I was given gifts that enriched my life. The next morning, after I had packed my bag and was getting ready to go to the closing session, I went back into the garden and sat down on the bench to look at the stubborn bud. It had opened and revealed a soft yellow rose. I bent down to look more closely at it and noticed around the stem a piece of plastic, a nametag. Ah, I thought, I have to know the name; perhaps I can get a rosebush like this. So I knelt down to brush the dirt off the plastic. A final gift for the week; the rose was named "Spirit of Peace."

## *A Holy Week Practice – Looking for the Helpers*
## *Saturday of Holy Week, April 11, 2020*

*On the day after the crucifixion of Jesus, the chief priests, fearful that the followers of Jesus might steal the body and claim that he had risen from the dead, asked for a guard to be set outside the tomb. Pilate agreed, and guards were set outside the sealed tomb on the Sabbath. But the women who had been at the Cross had seen the tomb and how the body was laid. They now waited for the Sabbath to be over so that they might treat it with spices, according to their custom. A hard part of being a helper is having patience, for not everything happens quickly even in the midst of a crisis. Who are the helpers you see practicing patience? Are you one of them?*

Posted Sunday, April 12, 2020

In 1992, I went to Menlo Park, CA, to attend a second conference with a group of Vietnam veterans who were also religious professionals. At the conference the previous year, I had, for the first time, actually spoken in some detail about my experiences in Vietnam. In doing that I had received so much relief that I was eagerly anticipating the coming conference. I had already made plans about what was going to happen, and it was all going to be good for me. I even had made a list of what I was going to do and the effect it would have on me. I had been asked to lead one of the evening worship services; I had really worked at the service and had created a combination of readings and music written by and for Vietnam veterans that I was sure was going to be an emotional high point for the group and for which I would humbly receive deserved praise. I was going to go to the nearby Pacific and walk out on the beach and figuratively let go of a bunch of stuff, freeing it to float into the sunset back to Southeast Asia; no longer would I have to carry those burdens. We were going to go the Menlo Park VA Medical Center which had established one of the first PTSD in-patient programs; I was going to find out when I could sign up for the program. And on the list went; I had high expectations. As soon as I arrived at the retreat Center, I did my perimeter walk, checking the boundaries and noting escape routes. Over the next couple days I implemented my pre-planned program. But . . . the tape recorder they provided for me to use to play the music didn't work well so everything got garbled up, and in the middle of the program one of guys got up to use the bathroom and slipped, falling on the marble floor, so the flow of my carefully planned service was broken. Then the trip to the Pacific didn't work at all; a strong wind blowing kicked up sand at the barren waste of the beach obscuring the horizon. And when we went to the VA and I asked the counselors about taking clergy into the program I was told, "Hell, no! They're too familiar with the treatment models and have such strong pre-set faith paradigms that they're impossible to work with." So all my plans were shot. A stone had rolled in my path. I settled in to endure the rest of the week. Then, unexpectedly, serendipitously, I began to receive gifts of grace (Each one has its own story!) that helped me see my way into the future. The first was the gift of using my voice to tell my story in light of my faith. The second was a gift of letting myself be present as a whole person, one that values all of my life as part of my story. And the third was the gift of accepting the help I needed to live fully. The helpers that gave me these gifts were Buddhists, followers of the Vietnamese monk Thich Nhat Hanh. And therein is a fourth gift – the practice of my Christian faith is enriched by the teachings of other faith communities.

## *A Holy Week Practice – Looking for the Helpers*
## *Easter, April 12, 2020*

*The women came to the tomb that morning and found the stone had been rolled away. They went and told the disciples who did not believe them, except for Peter, who ran to see the discarded linen cloths that had been around the body of Jesus. Luke then tells of two of the disciples who, while walking to Emmaus, a nearby village, were joined by a stranger. They shared with him the news of the disappearance of Jesus' body, their own shattered hopes, and the strange tale of the women. The stranger then interpreted these events in the light of the scriptures; so enthralled were the two disciples that they invited the stranger to stay with them. And so the stranger, as they prepared to dine, took the bread, blessed and broke it, and gave it to them. And their eyes were opened and they realized that the stranger was the Risen Lord Jesus. Sometimes it is indeed a stranger that helps us understand the gifts of life. Who have been the helpers that in your life have opened your eyes?*

## Afterthoughts

Even though the official "Easter" has passed, I am going to tie up a few loose ends. At the conclusion of the my Holy Week and Easter thoughts I wrote about four gifts of grace and parenthetically added that each had its own story. Though I have already written about these gifts in some of my books and on my webpage, I will add an explanation here as well.

The first of the gifts of grace was the ability to use my voice to tell my own story. At the time this gift was given I literally could not speak when I tried to tell my story. The year before, the first time I had gone to the meeting of clergy veterans, I had been able to get it out, but after that the emotions connected with my experiences still remained so strong that I was not able to manage a coherent narrative when I tried to speak. I had begun to be aware of this when

I was studying for my Doctor of Ministry Degree at Pittsburgh Seminary while I was taking a class about the writings of Reformed theologian Karl Barth. We were reading one of Barth's books, which were actually compilations of transcriptions of his lectures, and had come across a section addressing killing and war. Barth opined that for a Christian killing was wrong and pacifism was a correct stance. Having laid down the gold standard, so to speak, Barth then, in his typical fashion, waffled around allowing some exceptions that were still bad choices for a good Christian. While participating in a discussion on this reading with my classmates, all male Presbyterian ministers of whom only one other had been in the Armed Forces and I alone had been in a war, I grew increasingly agitated as I listened to the sterile opinions of those who had never had any experience of war or killing. Towards the end of the class, I blurted out, "You all have no idea what you're talking about!" Then I very bluntly told them I had been in Vietnam and that there were indeed cases when it might well be that taking a life was a good and righteous action. I spoke forcefully, and, though there were shocked faces, no one challenged me. After I spoke, the class for that day ended. Later that afternoon, the professor approached me and asked if I would say more on the following day. I agreed to do so. I had a sleepless night trying to sort out what I could say without revealing too much. I tried to give more perspective the next day and questions were being asked which threatened to take me into issues I did not want to discuss, and I became so overwrought that I finally said I just could not continue. So the class moved on to the next section of Barth while I sat in my seat and quietly tried to reassemble my shattered self. After the class neither the professor nor any of the other students spoke to me or expressed any concern. The next morning one of my classmates sat down to breakfast and I started to say something about the previous day's class and he stopped me. "I don't want to hear any more. I refuse to encourage your self-pity. Wallow away, but you can do it alone." And he got up and left. To say that my heart hardened would be an understatement. I retreated into the cold anger that had served me well and did not expose myself again to these good Presbyterians. However, the experience also froze my voice and I did not reveal the depth of my pain until the clergy conference of 1991. I have written of that "ambush" in other places; still, though I could start to speak, so powerful were the emotions associated with telling my story that I simply could not do it. However at the 1992 clergy veterans' conference I received the gift of voice by unwittingly ambushing myself.

Members of the Community for Mindful Living, followers of the teachings of the exiled Vietnamese Buddhist monk Thich Nhat Hanh, had been invited to meet with us to lead us in some meditation exercises. As part of their program they had brought with them a very nervous veteran who had a powerful story, but was fearful of telling it to a group of clergy; as he spoke he began to be overpowered by his emotions. At that point, one of the Community would strike a small "bell" she held in her hand, and he would pause, take a few deep breaths, and return calmly to the task at hand. I was very impressed, and during the question and answer period I affirmed his story saying how impressive it was to watch him, at the sound of the bell, gather himself and be able to continue on. I should have stopped at that point, but I went on to say how much I would like to be able to do that. The veteran looked at me and said, "Oh, you want the sound of the bell? Here it is; I give it you – now you will hear the sound of the bell calling you back to the moment and you can speak." As what he said hit me, the Community member with the bell came over and put the bell she had been holding in my hand, saying, "We believe in making things concrete as well. Now this is your bell."

I will pause in the story here to say that ever since then, when I speak on topics concerning my life, and when emotions begin to drag me back to the past and stir old reactions, I indeed hear the sound of a bell; and I can stop and take a few breaths, and come back to whatever I was doing and continue. It is not easy, and there is a lot more to the process of being in the present moment and dealing with emotions, but all the hard work is worth it because now I have my voice. I know it will be there, and I can tell my story.

Now the second gift is connected to the first. When the "bell" was placed in my hand, sitting on its pillow and with the small mallet or stick used to strike the edge of the bell, I just sat there looking at it. How long I sat there I do not know. The room was completely quiet as everyone simply looked at me. Finally, after a timeless eternity, I managed, I think, to say, "Thank you." And then things went on. Later one of the attending clergy told me that he wished they had a video going so I could see how long everyone just sat quietly looking at me, and so that I could see for myself the changes in expression that passed over my face. "It was like watching light break into the darkness," he said. Looking back on that experience and the experience of the previous year when I had told my story – the effect on some of the participants was profound, as I learned in later years – I began to become aware that one of the gifts I had (I think we all share this gift.) was the ability to just sit still and be a presence, letting others draw our of my silence what they needed at a particular moment. It is hard to convey exactly what I mean at this point. At our conferences, and in other gatherings, if I am going to say something I try to wait until the end because I know full well that often when I finish no one wants to follow me. Why is this? I know that I am a good speaker; I know that I am a powerful speaker. I have a way with words and images. And I speak from my own perspective and experience. Some have said what I say is often too personal or intimate, and others do not feel comfortable going there. Be that is as it may, I have become aware that the second gift is a consciousness of what simply one's witness and presence in a situation can mean. And if others can draw some strength or comfort by sitting quietly with me, so be it.

The third gift was given later in the day. I learned how to accept help when I needed it. I had never been reconciled to the reality that there were occasions when I needed to use the cane I had acquired in Vietnam. I resented the whole idea of using a cane for it forced me to reflect on things that I did not want to acknowledge.

But when challenged to create some form of meditation that would allow me to move slowly and purposefully, I discovered that this is exactly what the cane – my helper – would let me do.

The fourth gift reflects that elements of my healing journey have been brought about through the kindness of people who follow a different faith tradition then I do. Actually some of the healing journey has been made more difficult by Christians who do not have room in their belief systems for a God that works in a variety of ways in other peoples. I find my faith, which gives me stories and a language to express my own system of beliefs about the functioning and importance of relationships, allows me to appreciate the witness of other traditions.

# DISCUSSION SUGGESTIONS

WRITE IN THIS BOOK! Use a pen or pencil. Take notes if you have the book while you view the videos. Insert your own thoughts and ideas. After all, the purpose of the series is to free you up to talk about your emotions. Getting your thoughts on paper helps give them substance and reality, so write them down. There is a little room after the meditations, and there is always room in the margins!

When I started the **Emerging From Chaos** project, a video series (three introductory videos and 26 five-minute discussion starter videos) and this companion book, I reversed the usual course of events. I have never been able to do things in proper order, or so I have been told often enough. I had the idea for the series after having made a couple of video presentations for use during the chapel period here at Westminster Suncoast, the Florida Continuing Care Retirement Community (CCRC) where my wife and I reside, on the topic of "Coping With Crisis."

Our community chaplain knew of my background working with veterans suffering from Post Traumatic Stress Disorder, or Post Traumatic Wounds, as well as working with disaster relief teams after the participants would encounter the trauma of events such as Hurricanes Katrina/Rita or Gustav/Ike. He thought I might have some good thoughts to share with the community as we entered into the "trauma" of the COVID-19 pandemic. After all, with both an assisted living facility and a Health Care Center on our campus, we are ground zero for possible infection and transmission. I accepted the opportunity, as I wanted to help.

I used materials and thoughts that had been developed over the years as I worked as part of a leadership team offering retreats for war veterans and their partners. This developed into a larger ministry that touched victims of military sexual abuse and other trauma survivors. That program is described in another book.[1]

In the first video presentation prepared for my CCRC, I explained a pattern that I had heard and then expanded to create what I call the "trauma trail." I wish I could recall where I first heard the pattern, but I have attended so many workshops over the years and collected so much material that, when we downsized for retirement, I threw much of it away. Perhaps one of you reading this will recognize the pattern and can help refresh my memory so I can give proper credit!

At any rate, my expanded "trauma trail" pattern was as follows: In a TRAUMA one enter into CHAOS; feeling lost one seeks COMMUNITY; finding and greeting others and expressing mutual COMPASSION leads to forming a COVENANT around questions that, in the asking and discussion, lead to CLARITY about next steps and eventually movement out of the chaos into NEW LIFE. Having introduced this pattern in the first presentation, I went on to illustrate the pattern using an experience I knew would be common to all in the community.

In the second presentation, I spoke of the importance of discerning gifts that are received during the course of any trauma, the difference between a human "doing" and a human "being," and the importance of "spirituality." Having shared also the difference between a "discipline" and a "practice," I went on to share my own "spiritual practice."

As I thought about and organized these presentations, I realized that many in the community were experiencing the emotions that I had felt during my deployment in Vietnam. My experience at that time had been to discount those feelings, especially those arising

---

[1] **Hope and Healing for Veterans: Resources for the Spiritual Journey**. 2nd edition, 2015. Available through Amazon

from difficult events such as ambushes, abandonment, and sudden death. Those I stuffed away into a personal hidden compartment so I could get on with my life. This did not work well.

Long hours of counseling at the VET Centers in places where I have lived as well as retreats and conferences with other clergy veterans have moved me along the "trauma trail." Some of these experiences and my methods of dealing with the emotions of the "trail" are recounted in other books I have written. It did occur to me that I might have something to offer to help both the residents around me and their families avoid some of the problems I had encountered if I could encourage them to begin to address the emotions arising from the pandemic in a timely manner. Having used the alphabet technique before to help organize my thoughts I decided I would do so again.

Things I had learned over the years guided me. First, though each traumatic event has its own story, each also shares common points with other traumatic events: unexpected, sudden, destroying normal expectations, and so on. Along with the common points are common reactions: being overwhelmed, becoming angry, feeling alone, and so on. Thus I could share what I have learned from my experience and be a witness to the healing path. Another learning was the power of telling the story; I illustrated this in the first presentation I made. The third important point was to share the belief, drummed into me by a variety of counselors, that emotions are neither right nor wrong; they just are. It is how each of us addresses and manages the emotions that matter.

With this in mind I began to organize my alphabet and write short meditations. Over the years when I have started a project like this, a little inner voice has said, "You're going to be wasting your time!" I decided I would make that inner voice a part of my project so when I "set the stage" I introduced the one I am calling the "inner critic" as an important universal, though not always helpful, element of human life.

The video series contain three introductory videos and twenty-six five to six minute videos, one for each letter of the alphabet. Twenty-nine sessions! Who has enough time for that? Well, you can consolidate some of the sessions. However, let me remind you of the long time spent wearing a mask, washing your hands, and being socially distant. As I am writing this we are in our fourteenth week of "No Visitors" and staying on campus; that's 98 days. Multiply that by the number of hours in a day. If you have spent that much time living the pandemic and being a witness to events during the pandemic, you cannot expect to complete the hike on the "trauma trail" in a couple hours. This is not a stroll; it is a hike and there will be difficult stretches. You will need to take breaks. But don't give up; the view at the end of the trail of that promise of new life is amazing!

Describing and defining emotions I felt from the terribly dangerous pandemic was bad enough, but then eight minutes and forty-six seconds transpired on the streets of Minneapolis that exponentially increased the stress for all of us. I had already written and recorded a number of videos and had posted them on my YouTube channel. I paused and reviewed what I had said and what I had written and not yet recorded. I decided not to make any major changes for the pandemic itself had already revealed significant inequalities based on race and economic standing and what I had written about the pandemic trauma could also be read to apply to this highly public atrocity.

The one addition, and it was an important addition, was that I finally had a word, an emotion, I could use for the letter "X" – xenophobia.

In an early video I said that a book would be forthcoming and in it there would be questions that might be used to help guide discussions. As I began to formulate these questions, I discovered there was "a sameness" to what one might ask. Instead I have, after each segment, added a list of keywords drawn from what I said; it is up to the facilitators to decide whether to share these words before the segment is viewed or after or not at all. Also I have posed a question or two that could be asked based upon the groups I will describe at the end of this brief portion.

For any discussion group of any size there are a few general understandings about behavior and boundaries that should be set. First, any group, no matter what the size or who is included – even a base group of husband and wife – should be an intentionally "physically safe space." No weapons, threats, verbal intimidation, or harassment of any type can be tolerated. Now this does not mean a "safe space" in the sense that you are going to comfortable in the group discussions; you should not be. You are being given the opportunity, in the presence of respectful listeners, to talk about your own emotions and then to reflect upon how they are affecting your life. This will be risky and may well bring you to change some of the boundaries, beliefs and expectations you have long held. Such change is never comfortable and often not welcome.

The task of the one not speaking must be clearly defined as respectful listening; the one speaking has the floor without interruption. It should be understood that these gatherings are not therapeutic, but are offered to help people avoid therapy later in their lives. Certainly important group covenants would include display of mutual respect, compassionate understanding, and an agreement that what is said remains within the confines of the group, unless it involves an immanent threat.

Speakers might want to organize their thoughts using "Five W's and one H," that is the "who, what, where, when, why, and how" that make up a good story. When you read what I wrote about the letter "A" you can see that I addressed all six points in the first two short paragraphs. However, each person will have their own pattern of relating their experience; I offer this only as guideline.

Do not forget to write things in the book as they occur to you. Here are a couple of helpful hints to stimulate discussion. Do a word search – such as "anger in the Bible" or whatever books you may wish to use; "Shakespeare" or "the Koran" might be other choices. You will find a great number of references and maybe one will speak to you and spur your thoughts.

Or, read and write your own meditations to share with your group. Combine the two suggestions just made in some manner! It may not be easy; healing is hard work

To help each person discuss and evaluate how they chose to address an emotion, I suggest using what I am calling "push-pull" graphs. When I feel something strongly I find that I either "pushed" or "pulled" by that emotion, sometimes encouraged by my inner critic to go one way or the other. As I look back at an incident, I envision three graphs with me starting at a neutral point in the center. The first graph involves a physical reaction and the two poles are "Creative Activity" and Destructive Activity."

Creative _ _ _ _ _ _ _ _ _X _ _ _ _ _ _ _ _Destructive
Activity                                    Activity

The second graph notes the mental response and the two poles are "Engaged" and "Disengaged"

Engaged - - - - - - - - - - - X - - - - - - - - - - -Disengaged

The third graph charts spiritual positioning, and the two poles are "Change" and "Status Quo."

Change - - - - - - - - - - - - X - - - - - - - - - - -Status Quo

The questions I ask myself are "Where am I on this graph when the event occurs?" and "Where do I want to be now?" "What is the difference?" What is keeping me from moving?" "What does that say or mean to me?"

I would emphasize there are no "right" or "wrong" answers in this discussion; the goal is to better understand the emotion itself and how we reacted and how we would choose to react. You may find other graphs, or other words, or go in an entirely different direction. It does not matter as long as you keep talking and exploring.

As I went through my alphabet of emotions, I observed an interesting grouping of the various "emotions" that I will share with you. Again, your groupings might be entirely different. It seemed to me that my emotions could be grouped under four headings:

1. **Masking**, covering: meaning an emotion was hiding others or an emotion indicated a deep loss or a violated boundary
2. **Out of control**, no choice: meaning I was not in control of what happened
3. **Relationships**: meaning the emotion had some effect on family, friends, and associates
4. **Who am I**: meaning I lost my grounding in some way

And here is how the emotions divided out:

1. Anger, Jealousy, Sadness, Tempted, Wistful, Xenophobia
2. Boredom, Exhausted, Helpless, Isolated, Nervous, Overwhelmed, Queasy
3. Concerned, Guilty, Knowing, Labeled, Manipulated, Presence, Vulnerable
4. Depressed, Fear, Restless, Unknown, Yearning,

And one more, the final goal: enlightenment or wholeness – Zen

These groupings open another line of discussion that could be followed and I have added a question or two after each segment.

Now, go for it! But first, a word for those who are listening

# The Gift You Bring

IN THE PREVIOUS SECTION, you read this: the task of the one not speaking must be clearly defined as respectful listening; the one speaking has the floor without interruption.

Listening is very difficult in our world where, as we learn from our overuse of digital methods of communicating, we are ready to immediately express an opinion based not on any rational consideration, but solely on the basis of an emotional response. When we are tasked with siting quietly and listening we are simply not very good at it.

Let me remind you of the purpose of this study. It is to encourage people to tell their stories about the emotions aroused by the events that have occurred during this pandemic, and to explore, with the help of the gathered community, possible links to the greater stories of culture and faith. For this to occur requires an audience that is indeed listening respectfully. However, every listener has a natural disposition not to listen, especially if what is being said is somehow uncomfortable to hear.

Let's face it. There has been very little confortable about this COVID-19 pandemic. Our world has turned upside down in so many ways; expectations about living we accepted as the norm, or believed, or considered a social boundary have been upset; and we do not like it. Talking about how we feel about these changes is going to be difficult because sometimes our feelings are embarrassing. If that is not hard enough, then take into the account the eight minutes and forty-six seconds that have become an open wound to our nation's self-image and consider your own emotions when you are asked to consider such varied topics as "racism," "white privilege," "systemic

## Emerging from Chaos

racism," "reparations," and so on. Yet that is where we are and, if you have the courage to take the reality of all these broken and shattered norms, beliefs, and boundaries seriously, and are asked to listen rather than speak, and then to speak about your own emotions and perceptions, you can begin to imagine how uncomfortable this is going to be.

Here are a few hints to help you, the one who should be listening, discern if you are actually not listening.

If an inner voices say to you, "Do you remember when . . ." or "That sounds like the time when . . ," if you hear something similar to that, than you are not listening. Rather you have been reminded of an experience of your own, or even someone else, that is similar and you are now anxiously looking for an opportunity to grab the floor and tell your particular story because it is a much more illustrative and interesting story than the one the speaker is haltingly trying to share. And besides that, if you can start speaking that means you will not have to listen anymore!

If, upon hearing the speaker describes a situation, you say, "I know just what you should do," then you have fallen into the "problem solving" trap. Anxious to assist the speaker, your responses fall into three categories: "you should have," "you could have," or "if only you would have." While the speaker may be describing a difficult situation, and even though your suggestions may have merit, solving what you perceive as a problem has kept you from listening to what the speaker is saying about how he or she felt during the situation.

Along the same line, if you find yourself thinking, "that can't be right" or that is just wrong," then you have fallen into the trap of "judging." When you begin to define what the speaker is saying in terms of right and wrong, that means some understanding or perception you cherish has been challenged. Falling into the "judgment trap" allows you to stop listening as you consider what a proper sanction would be for the one who is "guilty."

If you find it necessary to ask someone to repeat what was just said, then you were not listening; your attention wandered away.

Now all of these, and there are other examples, are purely human reactions. Real, careful listening is risky; in the course of hearing someone speak, ideas may be expressed which are violent contradictions to those norms, beliefs and boundaries we had thought were settled truths.

So here is the general rule for responding during discussion that may follow. All of your sentences must begin with the word "I." Listeners, when responding, are simply not allowed to use the word "you." This will be difficult for each listener will actually have to think with some care about what she or he is going to say and how he or she will say it.

When I said that this would not be easy, I meant exactly that. Now begin. Remember all the videos associated with this series are freely available on YouTube.

# COPING WITH CRISIS

[These are the texts, slightly edited, of a two-part video presentation that I was asked to make during the time reserved for weekly chapel in our community.]

## **Presentation One**

*"For where two or three are gathered in my name, I am there among them.*
                                         *"*Matthew 18:20, (NRSV)

WELCOME TO WHAT I am calling my "Meditation Corner" here in our villa at Suncoast. I want to thank all of you who have told me that you are enjoying the cartoons and jokes about life during this pandemic that I have been putting on display outside the library. I glad you enjoy them because humor – laughter – is an important step as we hike along what I call the "trauma trail." I greatly enjoy it when I see a couple of you together laughing because humor is something best shared. As we know, where two or three are gathered together life seems richer, and the spirit rises.

My family and friends ask us, when they call, if we are all right. They know we chose to live in a community populated by the "vulnerable population." Recent news reports have emphasized that communities with a Health Center and assisted living facility can be "incubators" for contagious diseases. My response has to been to tell people that we are probably better off than they are. Let me tell you why.

There are a variety of ways to graph, outline, and evaluate specific traumatic events. Living through hurricane seasons in this age of tracking, watches, and warnings, we have all learned that hurricane pattern. Every traumatic incident is different, each one having its own story, it own timeline, its own impact. This COVID-

19 pandemic will have its own narratives. However, within any trauma, there exists a common arc of events as well as a common human experience of pain and despair, and also the possibility, the human dream, of creative activity and hope.

Think about the "trauma trail" as a long hike. We were thrown into this coronavirus pandemic and suddenly made aware that we were at risk. Without accurate information, without a treatment protocol, without a vaccine, everything seems out of control. However, in the midst of this CHAOS, we are already in a COMMUNITY, one that began to act with COMPASSSION in order to protect the weakest among us. Our relatives and friends may belong, as do we all, to a variety of communities – church, work, social, exercise, whatever. The difference is that we are in a community that actually lives together and we already have a COVENANT to stay together as we move through this pandemic.

We are in the midst of hiking the "trauma trail," and are, in truth, further along then most. As we move forward we are already discerning some CLARITY about the future, and eventually we will discover the unfolding promise of NEW LIFE. This pattern – CHAOS, COMMUNITY, COMPASSION, COVENANT, CLARITY, and NEW LIFE – is the "trauma trail."

To illustrate this I am going to fall back on the best teaching method I know, the one used by Jesus and many others. I am going to tell you a story.

As you listen, be aware of those moments when you can identify the CHAOS, or sense the COMMUNITY; take note of moments of COMPASSSION and how COVENANTS are created and implemented. Perhaps you may even identify some of the emotions aroused during the hike. Is some CLARITY found? Does the story end with NEW LIFE? You listen and you decide!

This is a story about a trauma we have all experienced – moving from one place to another! I am going to tell you about my parents' experience when they moved out of a manse into what our family called "our summer camp."

*********

I NEVER THOUGHT of my parents as romantic. Who does? But then my father retired, and my parents moved into the house in Maine, with its three porches. Located on a tidal creek, the old two-story, white house had six bedrooms, one bathroom, an outside shower, wood floors, no central heat, a pile of beach chairs and blankets and beach toys, and a multitude of floating items from rubber rafts to an old rowboat to a small sailboat. It had been a perfect retreat for spending long summer days. Minimal maintenance and a regular yearly painting schedule that managed to paint all twelve sides of the house every ten years kept it habitable and secure.

However, with Dad's retirement in view, the house had to be more then simply summer-habitable; my parents planned to live in it year round. Many planning discussions were held, but little preparation followed.

Then Dad's retirement parties took place; and, in the late summer, moving day arrived. My father and I rented a truck, packed everything into it, drove to Maine, and unloaded it all into the old house. Then, leaving my parents surrounded by furniture, boxes, and good intentions, I left to go back to the church where I was the pastor.

By the next summer when my family arrived for vacation, Mom and Dad had turned that "summer camp" into a comfortable home.

One night, at dinner, I asked them how they had managed this transformation.

"It was the three porches," my Dad replied.

"What?"

"Your mother's idea. She managed the whole thing."

## Emerging from Chaos

Putting down her fork, my mother took up the tale.

"Well, after you got the truck unpacked and all the furniture and boxes inside the house, you left! Now we appreciated the help, and we knew your time was limited, but we were not really prepared to face all that stuff alone. It didn't take us long to realize we were in a real mess. After all, the house had a lot of summer furniture in it. When we began to move that up into the attic we were reminded that the attic was already full of the furniture that preceded the summer furniture, as well as all your grandparents' stuff that we had never sorted through."

"Not to mention the stuff we stored up there over the years to just get it out of sight," Dad added.

"That's right, dear. Frankly, we were just completely overwhelmed!"

"And tired!" Dad interjected.

"Yes, worn out. So we left everything where it was and went to bed."

"Didn't look any better in the morning!" Dad joked.

Ignoring my father, mother resolutely plowed on.

"We spent the first day moving boxes around the house from one place to another, and then back again."

"The same with the chairs." Dad added.

"By day's end we hadn't even opened one box, and, on top of that, we were just plain old crotchety with one another."

Smiling at each other, they seemed to get lost in a shared memory of that conflict. So I prompted them. "What did you do?"

Dad responded, "We went out to dinner. All we had in the house was some bread and stuff for breakfasts and some peanut butter for lunch. We hadn't been to the store to get any groceries."

"And the kitchen was just a pile of boxes!" Mom added. "And after we came back to the house, we just sat and stared at the mess."

"Then we went to bed." Dad added. "I fell asleep, but she didn't!"

"No, I lay there thinking about the last couple days. I decided we needed to try something different. So the next morning I got up before your father, went down and made some coffee and toast, and when Dad came down I told him we were going to eat out on the front porch."

"Yup, we sat on the swing and ate and watched the squirrels in the maple tree across the street. After a bit your mother told me she had a proposition. So she propositioned me again."

Mother smiled at their old shared joke. She always said she could never get Dad to agree to anything unless she propositioned him.

"Yes, I suggested that after breakfast we go to the store and get some TV dinners and other necessities. Then we'd stop and buy some lobster rolls for lunch. And when we got back to the house we would clear out the front room altogether so we could have a place to sit. Then we'd have lunch out on the back deck."

"And that's what we did," Dad said. "Though at lunch, your mother started with phase two of her plan."

"It wasn't that I had everything all thought out! I just had a feeling that if we had meals at the house, something would happen. I simply suggested that we start by getting things that were important to us in place – for Dad, getting his books and papers as organized as he could; and, for me, getting that kitchen in some working order."

As Mom paused to breathe, Dad jumped in.

"We had decided that my study would be upstairs in the bedroom next to the one we use, so we went up to take look at the situation. Of course, being a bedroom, it had a bed in it! So we took down the bed and put it one of the three bedrooms you and your brother and your families fill when you come visit. We decided to use those bedrooms as a temporary holding area."

Mom's turn. "I also said that we wouldn't come upstairs without carrying something with us. I was thinking of Dad's books. When we went downstairs we opened one of the book boxes so we could carry a few every time we went up. Dad went to work on his study, and I worked downstairs in the kitchen."

Dad laughed. "That had an extra benefit: we weren't under each other's feet."

Mom continued. "We worked for a couple hours and then we took a little break for a snack and then spent another hour at it. Finally I prepared some TV dinners and suggested we eat out on the little back porch where we could see Dad's flower garden and catch a glimpse of the creek as well."

Dad smiled. "We just sat down, said grace, and ate our meal. Then we compared notes and made plans for the next day. Your mother insisted it start with breakfast out on the front porch."

Mom again picked up the narrative. "Then it just seemed more homey to have lunch on the deck and dinner on the back porch."

Dad spoke. "And we continued with that until it got too cold. But as soon as it warmed back up, we started doing it again." Thoughtfully, he continued, "Those three porches and those times doing nothing but being together reminded us of how much we had been through."

Mom added. "And gave us a chance to look ahead to all the things we wanted to do."

Dad was still thoughtful. "On those cool fall days in the morning we might wear mittens. Same at lunch." With a twinkle in his eye and looking at his wife, he went on, "But in the evening on the back porch, we would take a blanket and snuggle. When we're home alone, we still do!"

Mother blushed. I couldn't speak. Their love said it all.

\* \* \* \* \* \* \* \*

Well, that's the story. Did you notice the progression of the arc of trauma as my parents hiked that "trauma trail." The years had established a rhythm and an expectation about that house on the creek; it was a summer retreat. But now that rhythm was broken and the expectation was shattered; the house was not to be a hideaway, but a home.

This was the dream, but the reality snuck up on them. Quickly they found themselves overwhelmed, asking questions such as: "How did this happen?" "What will we do with all these chairs, these boxes?" "Where do we begin?"

They spent a day becoming more frustrated and grew angry at each other. They went out to dinner and came back to find that nothing had changed while they were out; no miracle had occurred. So they went to bed.

But my mother had an inspiration; they needed to eat breakfast together, somewhere familiar – the swing on the front porch. So they did – coffee, toast, watching squirrels, an old joke, a bit of humor, a proposition, a plan. They had formed a community – where two are gathered together, the spirit will work. They made a covenant together, just a small one – to buy food and have meals in their house. Lunch was shared in another sacred space, the back deck, where two or three could be together in peace, another small step.

During lunch, there was a compassionate question, "What do you need?" Dad needed his study and Mom needed a kitchen. A little bit of clarity began to develop. They went to work. The evening meal was shared in another sacred space, where two or three could gather – the back porch. Another covenant was made to visit the sacred spaces of their home daily: breakfast on the front porch, lunch on the deck, supper on the back porch.

Finally, did you hear the clarity that came to guide them? Placing the furniture or boxes, or having everything in place, were good steps, but what really mattered, and this became clear, was the relationship created over years together – the past, the present moment, and, yes. hope for the future – the new life to come.

Chaos, Community, Compassion, Covenant, Clarity, and New Life – this trail exists as any trauma unfolds.

Did you catch some of the emotions and negotiations in the story? There was a little bit of anger, some helplessness, frustration, but also there was some risk-taking, compromise, and laughter, understanding, respect, and love. A hike on the "trauma trail" brings out the full range of emotion. Now emotions are neither good nor bad; they simply are. It is how we choose to let the emotions guide life that matters. The question is do emotions control responses, or are emotions a call to consider creative responses? My parents' choice was to recognize the emotions and use them as a spur to negotiation.

Right now in this pandemic many are still in chaos, simply struggling to survive. However, in moving to a CCRC, we all chose to be part of a community. When the chaos of the pandemic hit, we did not have to search out and create a community to begin to take creative action. After the initial shock and confusion, the anxiety and fear, our community – administration, staff, and residents – began to take "compassionate" action in order to protect the health of the most vulnerable among us.

It was not easy – it never is – but together we moved forward. Masks have been made; schedules are being rebuilt in different ways. We have been pushed, learning new ways to communicate and to make better use of the technologies available to us. Most important of all and to our spirits, we have expressed our gratitude to one another in a variety of ways. When thanks are given, we know that God's spirit is working within us.

As together we hike along this "trauma trail," we have not yet achieved clarity about what is to come. There are still lots of bumps, stones, and pitfalls in the road ahead. What we do know is that we are moving into the new life together.

Until next session, I leave you with a pandemic blessing:

*When you meet a person with a mask,*
> *may you see the eyes of God's beloved child;*

*when you wash your hands,*
> *may you see the hands of God's beloved servant;*

*and when you maintain that six foot separation,*
> *may you bridge that space with a mutual blessing,*
>> *one both given and received,*
> *wishing good health to the one you meet upon the trail,*
>> *always looking for the gift that person brings to your life.*

# Presentation Two

*Now there are varieties of gifts, but it is the same Spirit . . .*
              I Corinthians 12:4, NRSV

*For I am longing to see you so that I may share with you some spiritual gift to strengthen you —or rather so that we may be actually encouraged by each other's faith, both yours and mine.*
                   Romans 1:11, NRSV

WELCOME BACK to my "Meditation Corner." Last week I shared with you a pattern outlining the common human response to a traumatic event. I called it the "trauma trail." Do you remember the pattern? A traumatic event occurs, and chaos quickly erupts. "What do I do?" "Where am I going?" Not wishing to confront such questions alone, I – or we – seek another person. Soon a community is formed within which questions like "Are you all right?" or "What do you need?" are asked. These compassionate questions elicit agreements, covenants, to work together. Small steps, little tasks achieved together, begin to lead to some vision about how to emerge from the chaos. Eventually, the community finds a pathway guided by more clarity to begin a new and different, hopefully enriched, life.

  Suncoast, I pointed out, had an advantage. When the rumored pandemic became a reality, we did not have to search for a community. We – administration, staff, and residents – are one, and together we were immediately in a position to ask compassionate questions and take actions to protect the vulnerable among us. So, we are further along the "trauma trail" then many and can begin to see some glimmerings about what the future may hold.

  As we wait for the new and different life, which we know is coming when this pandemic finally passes, I know I will be trying to discern what gifts have come out of all of this. It is a disquieting reality that every trauma changes society, offering the possibility of opening some new vista that may be life giving and bringing something new and different. After a war, battlefield practices have changed medical protocols; after a hurricane or flood, building codes are improved to mitigate damage from further storms. Even a personal tragedy may breed deeper self-awareness. So eventually we will see some gifts that may enrich our physical or mental or even spiritual journey. The Apostle Paul affirms that are a number of unexpected gifts that one may discover in oneself or in others.

Even though we are extremely fortunate to live in a community where we are committed to going though this COVID Crisis together, it is still not easy because while we – administration, staff and residents – are moving along, we are also hiking along as individuals, each one facing a different personal challenge. Think of the stories of individuals struggling following the Vietnam War, finally diagnosed years later with PTSD. It is easy to get stuck on that trail. I know because I have been on that hike and gotten stuck, more then once.

In any major upset, people offer helpful advice about how to fill time. We hear people affirm what they are doing during this lock down: listening to music, writing, sewing, experimenting with something, picking up a hobby long neglected, and so on. That's fine – people draw energy and comfort from different sources. A lot of this reflects the human need to be DOING something. However, going through a trauma is emotional, isolating, and exhausting leaving one worn out in body, mind, and spirit. Though we may have good intentions, rather then DOING, we often find ourselves just BEING – sitting, sleeping, eating, staring into space, losing track of time. Then we feel guilty because an inner voice tells us, "Darn it, I SHOULD BE DOING something!"

There are enough mandated things for us right now – washing hands, wearing masks, maintaining social distance – that we do not need our inner voice "SHOULDING" on us as well. First thing I would say to you is, "Give yourself a break!" This is a hard path we are hiking.

I want to share what I am doing as an individual to maintain my strength and balance as I hike this trail during this pandemic. To do this, I am going to use a portion of the presentation that I made when I led healing retreats for war veterans and their partners. This segment was titled "A Spiritual Life That Works." Notice I do not say "A Christian Spiritual Life" or "A Buddhist Spiritual Life." In these retreats we had veterans and partners coming from a variety of "spiritual" backgrounds and we leaders were attempting to talk about "spirituality" as inclusively and broadly as we could. I have adapted this presentation to use with victims of sexual assault as well as with those deeply affected, both victims and relief workers, by natural disasters such as hurricanes or floods.

First, here is definition for spirituality I have used with young people going through confirmation. **SPIRITUALITY** is a life-long journey (not a one shot and you've got it) of human experience of the whole human person (both the good and the bad; no part-person spirituality) shared with others and self, which is valued through the intimate relationships formed. I would stop at this point and, without fail, some young person would say, "You haven't mentioned God in your definition." I'd reply that there were lots of spiritualties that did not include God, but if we wanted God in our lives then we could invite God to be part of our "human experience . . . " through that relationship "shared with others."

During any trauma, as I said, memorable phrases pop up: "This won't last forever!" or "Stay safe!" or "Keep busy!" A few come up that speak of spirituality: "We are spiritual beings having a human experience." or "The Lord is my strength and my shield . . ." or "Adversity opens our eyes to a need that is higher than our own strength." or "Who can add one hour to life by worrying? Since you cannot do this little thing, why worry about the rest?"

There is a lot of truth in these phrases. They express a yearning for that mystical presence faith proclaims, that spirituality, that relationship with some power greater that is comforting, accessible, present, believable, full of hope, and capable of healing.

## Emerging from Chaos

Now no matter how much we retreat leaders tried to distance ourselves from our own religious heritage and speak of spirituality in broad terms, honoring and affirming the vast variety of faith traditions with the differing disciplines, eventually we were asked, "Well, what do you do?"

Nothing like being put on the spot! However, the leadership team, having preached openness, tried to answer as honestly as we could. This was my answer.

I wanted a spiritual program so I could, if all went well, say to myself at bedtime, "Boy, I had a good day!" As a pastor I knew all about the disciplines recommended for a "healthy spiritual life." Things like daily prayer, daily Bible reading, time set aside for reflection and praise, self-sacrifice, regular confession and self-examination, and the list goes on.

No matter how much I would try to follow these disciplines, I would fall short, usually simply running out of time. Thus, at the end of many days, I would feel I had failed. I SHOULD have done better.

So I took a hard look at the "spiritual disciplines." Daily Bible reading? I have slogged through the Bible book by book and there is plenty of it that I never want to nor need to see again. I think particularly of sections of *Leviticus* or *Numbers*!

Self-sacrifice? I am afraid the way it is practiced by most religious professionals means that what is sacrificed is one's family time and relationships; here I speak from ample experience!

So I "designed" a program of spiritual PRACTICES that at least give me a chance to feel good at the end of each day. I do not believe that I can separate my physical well being from my spiritual well being, so my program addresses both sides with a daily practice of three things I must not do and three I must do. The three "must not's" are on the physical side: **Do not hurt anyone! Do not hurt myself! Do not give up on community!** Simply explained, I was trained really, really well in the use of violence, so well that it was the "go to" response, either verbally or physically. So disheartening was this tendency to violence that, at one point, in order to protect the ones I loved, my base community, I isolated myself from them by participating in various forms of self-destructive behavior. Thus the three "do not's" that help me affirm the importance of community, being connected with others.

The three "must do's" are on the spiritual side as they specifically affect relationships. Right now, this part of my practice has problems – and you'll know why immediately. ***Do smile! Do hug someone!*** Pandemic problem! Masks hide smiles and social distancing means no hugging! So how do I address this? Well, if I cannot see smiles, I can hear laughter. I can see people with their shoulders shaking. That is one reason I put up those jokes outside the library – to encourage laughter. Now the hugging – that is more difficult. The inability to physically touch another human being is the greatest loss in this pandemic. Think of the powerful images over the years of people simply holding hands. And we cannot do this. Oh, I can pet various animals, and that is comforting, but it is not the same. And I can hug Ann, but still that is not the practice. I did find a partial answer. As a human and spiritual practice I meditate. Through meditation I free my spirit to travel to touch others.

The third "must do" is ***Do say "Thank you!" to someone***. The first two – smiling and hugging – are the very essence of what it means to be in community with others; the last defines what I think the Apostle Paul uses as the basis of spreading the good news, the mission, by expressing gratitude to others for the gifts they bring to enrich our lives.

These "do's" and "don't" cross over. My spiritual practice of hugging is also a physical practice; incidentally, I always seek permission before I hug. Respecting personal space is both a physical practice as well as a spiritual statement I make about another person's value as a child of God.

My entire spiritual program is something I do by choice. I "designed" it myself so no one is "shoulding" on me! There is nothing more deadening to the soul than a "spiritual advisor" who says you "should" do this!

The rewards of my spiritual program are always unexpected. This was difficult for me as a veteran for my term for an unexpected event is an "ambush." I did not enjoy being ambushed; I responded violently. I did not deal well with the unexpected, but then I asked myself what is expected in life: death and taxes. We expect trouble, live in fear of it, and set ourselves up for misery. I decided it would be better to expect happiness, so I am open to being surprised by the gifts Paul advises us to look for and appreciate being ambushed by joy.

The simple "do's" and "do not's" of my program are deeply spiritual practices, not disciplines. Remember: a discipline is a set-up program one aspires to achieve; a practice is how one actually lives.

There it is. Three "do's" and three "do not's." I have days when I can look at what occurred and say, "Boy, I had a good day!" Then there are times when I miss the mark, but not many. I commend to you the joy of developing your own spiritual practices that will feed your soul and bring you strength upon the hike. Especially be looking for gifts.

I leave you with a pandemic blessing:

*When you meet a person with a mask,*
    *may you see the eyes of God's beloved child;*
*when you wash your hands,*
    *may you see the hands of God's beloved servant;*
*and when you maintain that six foot separation,*
    *may you bridge that space with a mutual blessing,*
        *one both given and received,*
    *wishing good health to the one you meet upon the trail,*
    *always looking for the gift that person brings to your life.*

Emerging from Chaos

# SETTING THE STAGE

AS WE EMERGE from this pandemic, our work to find our new, healthy "normal" will be just beginning. Perhaps a vaccine has been created, or, at least, an effective treatment protocol. Hopefully, both!

Certainly we anticipate the joyful task of reuniting with families and friends and others in the various communities to which we belong and where we live. Those times of getting together will be full of laughter and joyous tears. However, not all these reunions will be happy occasions; many memorial services will be held for those who died during the pandemic and for whom services were not held. There is a lot of "disenfranchised grief" that needs to be addressed. Finding the new "normal" is going to be a hard task.

We have all been affected by this pandemic. Just think of how our national perception of who is important and who is not has been challenged. "Essential workers" were not the richest, or best paid, or most highly trained among us. Highly trained, professional, wealthy individuals, ranging from sports stars to business leaders to organizational executives, were deemed "non-essential" and told, "Stay home!" As we search for a new "normal" one of the questions to be debated is whether a "non-essential person" like a baseball star or a football player or a business or non-profit executive should be paid huge sums while those deemed to be "essential" during this pandemic often have to work two jobs in order to survive.

To this pandemic, with all of its unknowns, had been added a new, terrible dimension. Living as we are in this age of digital communication, we receive "breaking news" quickly. Xenophobia and racism have long accompanied any trauma. In the story of the Good Samaritan, we see people pass by a wounded individual. The shocking twist in that story is the person who does stop is from a marginalized community.

In the earliest days of this pandemic, it was called the "China flu." Disease knows no national boundaries and this misguided labeling gave permission to scared individuals to terrorize a segment of our nation's population. We have seen this xenophobia morph into racism of the worst kind. Riots have broken out in our cities, triggered by repeated incidents of racist brutality carried out under the old mantra of "law and order."

The digital revolution has, however, brought us something else new. Courageous people are now taking videos using their cell phones. The visual evidence provided has shown that the old excuse for brutality, "resisting arrest," just will not hold water anymore. Part of the pandemic trauma is the reality of these incidents; and as we watch on our various devices, we pay an emotional price that will have to be addressed.

There are difficult discussions coming about our social covenants and understandings. While these are taking place, the pain of individuals needs to be addressed as well.

So I want to share with you some thoughts about how trauma and emotions and feelings can affect each of us. What I offer is based upon my experience of helping lead healing retreats for deployed veterans and their partners as well as my own long search for healing from the trauma and losses of my war in Vietnam, a decades long story of discovery, recovery, and new life.

I do this hoping to encourage we who are now "pandemic veterans" to enter into serious discussions about how our physical, mental, and spiritual well-being has been affected by this experience and to have these discussions in a timely manner, rather then putting them off for decades and letting the unaddressed, unnamed emotions fester, causing other problems down the trail.

Let me set the background for what I am doing.

We are all born with an inner critic. At birth, the critic has a lot of power over us and how we act, for we have not yet learned any boundaries.

It takes a while to begin asking those critical questions that will guide development: "Is this worth a full blown tantrum, or will a simple whimper suffice?" "What are the possible results of this activity? Will it feel good or will it hurt?" Our earliest boundaries are quite transactional as all evaluation is aimed at satisfying our own perceived needs. This is a healthy process and eventually we confront more complex boundary questions that help us to set limits on our emotions as we pursue our daily lives. This is frustrating to our inner critic who no longer so completely controls our activities. We have learned how to make choices.

It is then that our inner critic begins to find its annoying voice and changes tactics. Without the power to initiate immediate action, that inner critic turns to evaluating our daily actions and sharing its evaluation with us. Sometimes that inner voice asks questions: "Are you sure you want to do this?" Sometimes doubts are raised: "Perhaps you should read the directions?" Sometimes it offers advice: "You can drive through this water!" "You don't need to check. It's safe to dive!" While one has to pay attention to that inner voice, the value of its advice must always be assessed for often the advice is based more on emotion than rational thinking.

And after anything we do, no matter how well that action or performance has gone, that inner voice can be counted on to say: "You should have done better!" or "If only you could have . . ." or "If only you would have . . ." Our inner critic rarely delivers a supportive message, preferring to undercut us with a "should'a, would'a, could'a" put down that brings up a variety of emotional responses. Emotions are what feed the power of the inner critic, and that inner critic is not a fair evaluator.

Remember: emotions are neither right nor wrong; they just are! What matters is how we confront, accept, and handle these emotions. The touchstone I use is to ask whether or not the inner voice is leading me to act in a way that would be somehow destructive rather than in a manner that possibly could be creative.

However, all boundaries and expectations and negotiated relationships are thrown out when something traumatic happens. A hurricane or a tornado, a wildfire or an earthquake occurs and the "normal" is destroyed. Emotions rise, and the inner critic has a field day. I have been down that pathway! In order for me to recover, to establish what my new "normal" would be, I needed some person or some group that could listen with respect, the courage to tell my own story, and a greater story with which I could connect my personal story.

Here is what I am going to offer. I am going to take the 26 letters of the alphabet and assign to each a word describing or eliciting an emotion or feeling starting with that letter. Then I will link to each letter a story or thought touching on that emotion from a greater story to which I might be able to link my own personal experience. Since I am from the Judeo-Christian tradition I will make references to the Bible; however, other traditions have similar stories within their histories that can be used just as well.

My alphabet of emotions is by no means comprehensive; it only reflects the emotions with which I have struggled.

Who is going to listen to all this? Well, you can, if you wish, because for each letter I have created a YouTube video. You can use the videos as discussion starters within your own family or community. Assemble a small group, begin, and continue the discussions. Perhaps together you can create your own individual alphabets of emotion. Do not wait. Jump in now and start!

Having said that, the first video begins with the letter *A*.

Emerging from Chaos

*Anger*
*Boredom*
*Concerned*
*Depressed*

# A

## ANGER

*I am utterly spent and crushed; I groan because of the tumult of my heart.*
Psalm 38:8, NRSV

A PTSD BUDDY really loves Psalm 38. My buddy is a Catholic nun, who served in communications in Vietnam; she found a translation of this verse that reads something like this, "I roar with anguished heart!" I like that as well.

I remember the first time I was ambushed in Vietnam. My first reaction was a "What the hell?" panic, followed by a fearful "Oh My God!!" which immediately transformed into a profane, white hot rage, and I attacked literally roaring a battle cry of "#%#&#!!" I survived; some of my companions, but not all, survived. The attackers did not. The anger, the rage, saved me, pushing me beyond what I ever imagined I could do.

Here's the upside of anger: it will help you survive because it masks, makes inaccessible, all other emotions. The downside is that consistent anger, roaring, or as other Bible translations put it, "deep groaning," can become an easy escape from the hidden, deeper emotions so that they are not named, or recognized, or confronted, or addressed, but left to fester within the human soul as untreated wounds.

My anger at the ambush was triggered because it, with sudden brutality, shattered boundaries that I had learned over the years: "One fights fairly, if one fight at all." "Thou shalt not kill." Others followed; they fell quickly. "Only 'adults' fight in wars." Anger enabled me to survive, but years later it drove me close to suicide.

The boundaries that were violated were good, useful, important, mutually shared expectations that made "normal" life possible in the society in which I existed, but that unexpected incident, the ambush, destroyed that "normal" forever. The anger that completely possessed me was not, however, the emotion that was most deeply felt. The emotion that was hidden, masked, by the anger was a deep, profound sadness that the "normal" I had known, the one that defined good and evil, and gave life meaning, was gone. And I did not know what was going to replace it.

This pandemic of coronavirus, when first rumored, was going to be easily controlled. Well, that expectation was quickly shattered. COVID-19, at it came to be known, gained a foothold and took off, striking the most vulnerable among us as well as those who tried to render aid and assistance. There was not enough protective equipment, not enough information; no one seemed to know what was happening, except people were dying in large numbers and alone. Those rendering emergency aid, working in the hospital emergency rooms and wards, maintaining the equipment and rooms, feeding the staff and patients, these "essential workers" were not immune to the ambush of an unseen enemy. The toll of death among them rose, and the survivors have not yet begun to face the future. Unfocused anger roared at politicians, at leaders, at organizations, at mayors, at governors, at doctors, at whoever could be found to blame or shame, the two allowable, safe, but still destructive actions of anger.

But these reactions do NOT recognize or attempt to name the masked emotion of sadness. Without giving that masked emotion its proper place, without honoring the true reality of the hidden feeling, no steps towards healing or finding any pathway to a new "normal" can begin. There only exists a continuing spiral of meaningless reactions that lead to self-destruction.

**Keywords:** ambush, panic-fear-rage, boundaries, normal, masked

What have you lost that angered you? Did you recognize that loss at the time?

# B

## BOREDOM

*For everything there is a season, and a time for every matter under the heaven: a time to be born, and a time to die; a time to plant, and a time to pluck up what is planted; a time to kill, and a time to heal; a time to break down, and a time to build up; a time to weep, and a time to laugh; a time to mourn, and a time to dance; a time to throw away stones, and a time to gather stones together; a time to embrace, and a time to refrain from embracing; a time to seek, and a time to lose; and time to keep, and a time to throw away; a time to tear, and a time to sew; a time to keep silence, and a time to speak; a time to love, and a time to hate; a time for war, and a time for peace.*

Ecclesiastes 3:1-8, NRSV

NO ONE EVER contemplated that our mobile society would be frozen in mass immobility. Even the well-known passage from Ecclesiastes, one that became a popular song back in 1960's (*Turn! Turn! Turn!* by the Byrds), asserts that life will be full of a variety of activities. The passage does not say there will be "a time for being locked down and doing pretty much nothing." Dreams of vacation were phrased in terms such as "I don't want to do anything except . . ." and then the hopes would follow: go to the beach, visit the old folks at home, spend time with the family, go to a favorite spot, and so on. The phrase never said simply, "I don't want to do anything."

In the midst of any action during my time in Vietnam, boredom was not a problem. A quick firefight, a period standing watch, a patrol, all these demanded that one be alert and attentive; to lose focus meant death.

However, there did exist a lot of "down time," and those in charge recognized this. Therefore formal distractions were provided through the USO, libraries of various sorts, various rank-based clubs, in-country R&R opportunities, as well as opportunities to study to advance in rank. When formal distractions proved inadequate, warriors were adept at finding other kinds of distractions. There is a human need to ward off boredom, of not having anything to do. If all else failed, one could simply go for a walk around the base.

However, this "pandemic lock down," with its "14-day quarantine" provision for many, has changed all that. Faced with the loss of travel, mass cancellation of events that mark the rhythm of life (graduations, baptisms, funerals, holidays, sport seasons, and so on), and warnings to wear masks, wash hands often, and maintain six feet of separation, people responded as best they could. Good intentions were announced loudly, ranging from learning a new language, completing home improvement projects, taking part in volunteer activities such as making masks, starting a new exercise program, and so on.

However, the reality is that eventually everyone succumbs to a feeling of ennui, that tiredness that leads to longs naps, self-indulgence, and self-pity. The scale, the recycling bin of empty bottles, and inability to recall what day it is reinforces the reality that one is perhaps not doing well with this boredom.

The plain, hard truth is that this immobility and isolation is hard work, exhausting to the body, mind, and spirit. And no one, least of all, your inner critic, that nagging little voice, is willing to give you a break!

**Keywords:** immobility, down time, good intentions, self-indulgence, Isolation

What did you miss most that you could no longer do? Why?

Emerging from Chaos

# C

## CONCERNED

*And whoever does not provide for relatives, and especially for family members, has denied the faith and is worse than an unbeliever.*

I Timothy 5:8, NRSV

PAUL WRITES TIMOTHY with blunt advice about the expected behavior of those who would follow Jesus. Looking past the harsh phraseology, what Paul writes reflects the reality common to us all; we are concerned for the welfare of our family members. It not only parents who wonder about the status of children, whether far away or nearby, but the children worry about the parents. Living in a senior retirement community with both an assisted living facility and Health Care Center, I can hear the concern in my own children's voices as they ask, "Are you all right?" As parents having children living at a distance, my wife and I ask them the same thing. We want to go help as they face home-schooling and childcare concerns, but we are helpless. We have no way to travel that distance. And then, given the concerns about transmission, would we have to do a 14-day quarantine before we could see them? And where would we do that?

So we use our modern version of letters to communicate: Skype and Facebook, Zoom and Twitter. The fleeting images and words, subject always to the wireless connection strength, are not as satisfying as a real, tangible letter that can be held, re-read, and returned to, even when the wireless connection fails, or the power goes out, or the years go by.

As senior citizens, part of the "vulnerable" population, we are concerned about the health and wellbeing of coming generations as we see society in turmoil, concerned about buying food, paying rent and other bills, about education, job loss and about future employment. And if we survive, will we have the financial resources

Emerging from Chaos

to maintain our living standard in the new "normal" of life?

Yes, make no mistake about it! We are also concerned for ourselves! If we were to catch this COVID-19, would we survive? After all, we are that segment known as the "vulnerable elderly." And, even though our community has instituted actions to protect us from infection, we all know that will not happen. In our hearts, we recognize that all this hand washing, mask wearing, and social distancing is buying time for society: hoping that medical facilities will not be overwhelmed, waiting expectantly for an effective treatment protocol, and praying for development of a vaccine.

Also we are concerned that our worldview of a society that believes in freedom and liberty, justice and fairness, equality and access, our dream of a nation is being shattered. Along with that worldview goes a faith in a Creator that wishes good for creation, and we, confront once more the age old question, "How can a loving Creator allow bad things to happen to good people?"

All these concerns come shouting in the night. But no answer comes.

**Keywords:** family, future, finances, buying time, worldview shattered

How have your relationships changed? Do you feel closed to anyone?

# D

## DEPRESSED

*So I became great and surpassed all who were before me in Jerusalem; also my wisdom remained with me. Whatever my eyes desired I did not keep from them; I kept my heart from no pleasure, for my heart found pleasure in all my toil, and this was my reward for all my toil. Then I considered all my hands had done and the toil I had spent in doing it, and again, all was vanity and a chasing after wind, and there was nothing to be gained under the sun.*

Ecclesiastes 2:9-11 NRSV

IF YOU ARE NOT feeling depressed, let me help you. Here are a few of the symptoms: feelings of sadness or helplessness; irritability and frustration over small matters; sleeping too much; changes in routine activities; small tasks take more energy; weight gain or weight loss; anxiety; fixating on the past; trouble thinking or concentrating.

And, if that wasn't enough, here are some of the symptoms of depression specific to older adults: memory difficulties, physical aches or pains, fatigue, loss of appetite, sleep problems, and staying at home (rather than going out to socialize or do something new).

Now are you depressed? Or are you simply disgusted? After all, this pandemic is forcing us to actually live so many of the symptoms that it is hard to differentiate depression from our new daily living!

In the story above we find that ambitious manager or worker who, having enjoyed his years of labor and made careful plans, finds that all he had done was blow away by the winds of fortune and all that he had accomplished was meaningless. In other words, the poor soul has lost a sense of who he was, the satisfaction of the role he had filled in life, and discovered that all he had done had no meaning!

Herein we find three real clues to help evaluate whether or not one is truly depressed. Here I will speak personally of my own treatment path and observations I made as an "informed consumer."

Coming out of a traumatic experience, in my case, war, I had lost a sense of self-worth, of personal identity. To re-establish that I had to answer the question "Who am I?" his meant delving into my past and talking about the identity I had before the trauma, or thought I had, and what had caused a change in that perception. This was hard work.

Then I had to discern what my role was by asking "Who am I with others?" I had taken on so strongly the role of warrior, a destroyer, that I was having trouble laying down that role, one that did not translate well into society. So I had to explore new roles that I could assume that would help define creative and healthy relationships. This also was not easy.

Finally I had to ask, "What do I do now?" I had to find some activity that gave my life a discernable meaning. I found this through several roles that I took on: husband, father, pastor, and grandfather, among others.

This was my healing trail out of the diagnosis of depression that I had received when I was diagnosed with Post Traumatic Stress Disorder. Let me add that we are in the midst of the pandemic trauma and what there is certainly a lot of depression connected with it, the operative word for my diagnosis was "post." Having not dealt with the problem at the time, I got caught in having to deal with it later. If, for example, in five years when we have achieved a new "normal" and everyone else is going into stores or stadiums freely, but you find yourself staying at home, wearing a mask in the house, only going out in the dark in night to empty stadiums or stores, then we need to talk about your post traumatic depression. I hope you avoid that by discussing NOW the emotional price you have paid during this pandemic!

**Keywords:** living the symptoms; self worth, roles, meaning, healing trail

Is this all worth it? Am I doing any good for anyone?

# E

## EXHAUSTED

*Once when Jacob was cooking stew, Esau came in from the field, and he was exhausted. And Esau said to Jacob, "Let me have some of that red stew, for I am exhausted!" ... Jacob said, "Sell me your birthright now." Esau said, "I am about to die; of what use is a birthright to me?" Jacob said, "Swear to me now." So he swore to him and sold his birthright to Jacob. Then Jacob gave Esau bread and lentil stew, and he ate and drank and rose and went his way. Thus Esau despised his birthright.*
Genesis 25:29-34, English Standard Version (ESV)

DECADES AGO, exhausted by the activities of "hell week" at the fraternity to which I was pledged, I was ready to give up and walk away. A couple of brothers, noticing my distress, pulled me aside. I fully expected I was going to be subjected to some new form of harassment, but one of them said, "We want you to have a few moments to calm down." No one spoke for a few moments; for me, it was a relief just to be sitting quietly. Then one of the brothers spoke, "We know you're exhausted and on edge, but we want you to stick it out. Here's the deal, before you make any decisions about the future, tell someone you want to talk with us." I was surprised; someone cared. So I endured and became a brother, a privilege I have never regretted. I learned then that it was not a good idea to make any decision when physically or mentally or spiritually exhausted. Rather then decide I had to endure.

Too bad Esau didn't have someone to pull him aside. I wonder what the story would look like if he had been encouraged to endure his hunger and brush off his little brother's greed. However, no one pulled him aside, and Esau made a decision he came to regret.

In our current pandemic lock down, we are enduring in spite of the creeping exhaustion of having been in this status for several weeks. It has been an extended "hell week." Our mobility is limited;

we have various "to do's" such as wearing masks and washing hands; and we feel a bit put upon. And in some way this is our own fault. We have done this to ourselves. After all, we live in community, and the administration has emphasized that living in community means accepting that we have a responsibility to and for one another. Thus we "agreed" to stay on campus for the duration of the pandemic period, leaving rarely only for truly necessary items. We also agreed that, for the safety of the community, we would not receive any visitors and would, if we left to go to a doctor's appointment, submit to a re-entry protocol to get back on campus. We recognize this; but still, implementing the various agreements is exhausting. We have to remember to put on and carry a mask with us, to continually wash or sanitize out hands, and to maintain the six feet of separation. All of this takes some focus and energy as it is a new way of doing things, a change, and no one likes to change. Mix in with this our worries about our families and friends, our next meal, and our next round of bills, and we begin to understand why we are on edge.

We are exhausted!

**Keywords:** on edge, enduring, to do's, focus, worries

Has anyone helped lighten your burden? How? Have you tried to help someone? How?

# *F*

## FEAR

*In that region there were shepherds living in the fields, keeping watch over their flock by night. Then an angel of the Lord stood before them, and the glory of the Lord shone around them, and they were terrified. But the angel said to then, "Do not be afraid; for see, I am bringing you good news of great joy for all people..."*
Luke 2:8-10, NRSV

WHEN I SPOKE ABOUT the letter *A,* I told the story of the first time I was ambushed. If you recall I spoke of three reactions: first was a "What the hell?" panic, followed by a fearful "Oh My God!!" which immediately became a battle cry of "#%#&#!!" This is what I call the warrior response to an attack: if one is fortunate, one goes through panic and fear to that anger that will ensure survival.

The story today tells what we may call the shepherd response: an unexpected appearance accompanied by a great light (that must have been a bit shocking) followed by fear, but then, rather than an attack, a clarifying message, to which the shepherds responded by having a discussion about the instructions given, and, out of perhaps curiosity, decided to follow the directions to discover if the promised miracle was so.

What will be the story told about our pandemic response, one still being written? Which one of the following will it be? Or will it be something entirely different?

Will we make the warrior response, attacking those who seem to bring the ambush to us?

Or will we make the shepherd response, and form a committee to discuss whether or not we will do anything at all, and if so, what?

Or will we recognize the problem – an infection – that has caused plenty of panic, and adopt an attitude of fear, thinking magically that we can stop the spread of the disease by locking our doors, hiding our faces behind masks so our emotions cannot be seen, avoiding human contact as if others are lepers, and rearranging our lives so we six feet apart from others, and adopt that as a new "normal?"

Or will we recognize the problem – an infection that is caused plenty of panic, adopt temporary measures to slow the inevitable spread of the disease giving medical professionals and scientists adequate time to develop treatment protocols and perhaps a vaccine, and the, with determination, set our goal as coming to a new "normal" that accepts the reality of various societal changes in preparation, medical care, relationships, movement, and remuneration while setting the goal of affirming the human dream to assemble freely, without hiding our faces, and greeting one another with a human touch of respect and affection?

That third choice, to live in fear, is to exist under a tyranny defined by others, to barely survive, to be blown about by the whims of power. This is neither the dream which motivates America or any free people, nor is it the ultimate goal of any creative faith community.

I prefer the last choice, though it may be stated in other ways with slightly different outcomes. However, to live in hope, and joy, and freedom requires courageous people who choose courageous leaders, something we currently do not have.

My choice is not to live in fear, but to move forward with determination. There will be a price to be paid, but so be it.

**Keywords:** response, panic, inevitable spread, tyranny, courageous

What is behind the fear? Is something broken or lost, or do we worry about losing something?

# G

## GUILTY

*I will get up and go to my father, and I will say to him, 'Father I have sinned against heaven and before you; I am no longer to be worthy to be called your son; treat me like one of your hired hands.'*

Luke 15:18, NRSV

HERE I AM on familiar ground. Lord knows my life through my schooling and in the Navy would qualify me in many ways as "the prodigal son." When I announced to my parents I was going to seminary, their reaction was, "You! You're kidding?" My grandmother's reaction, along the same lines, prompted her to write a letter of apology for when she first heard she thought it was all a joke. And my inner critic, that inner voice, assured me I was going to make a fool of myself.

That inner critic had never been shy about making me feel guilty. From early schooling on through high school, I lived in guilt for not having done enough studying ("You should have gotten a 100% on that test rather then a measly 92%.") to guilt for doing something I ought not to have done ("You shouldn't have had that second glass of wine, let alone the first one!"). My sins of omission and commission kept that inner voice constantly yapping at me. Though I had become rather good at committing the various offences, I was not as successful at ignoring the accumulated guilt and became a relentless seeker of forgiveness through nightly prayer rituals which today would earn me a diagnosis of "obsessive compulsive." I would have been a good Roman Catholic.

My penchant for succumbing to temptation during my college days and my fraternity years did not lessen. And when I went into the Navy and went to Vietnam even my inner critic gave up bothering me about what I was doing.

Only after I came home did that inner voice wind up again

having discovered a new burden to load on me called survivor guilt. "You should have died with them!" "You don't deserve to be here." That inner voice, I thought, had a point. And I struggled for years until I made peace with living.

And now we have the pandemic, and my inner critic is at it again. I stop at Dunkin' Donuts for coffee. "What if that cup is carrying the virus? Didn't you just wipe your lips? How can you go back home without going into quarantine?" I listen and get angry with myself for having displayed poor judgment and given in to temptation again.

I go to the post office to mail some documents and come home to work at the computer. And then the inner voice speaks, "You forgot to wash your hands when you came in! Now you have to disinfect everything you touched? Do you remember where you went? Are you sure you got it all?" I listen and I become frustrated that I have forgotten the ritual and No, I do not recall every spot I touched!

Even the final card is played. "Did you see today's death count? Why are you not a statistic as well?" That inner bastard is relentless.

But, for me, guilt is an old companion. And, in a few minutes, I am able to evaluate the accusations, run my "repair tapes" as I call the process, and place whatever the event was in a proper context over against the totality of the gift of living.

The inner critic was right about something. It told me I would, by going to seminary and going into the ministry, make a fool of myself. I have done so; for Christ's sake, I have done so. And I don't regret it one bit.

**Keywords:** fool, survivor guilt, omission and commission, "repair tapes," gift

What have you done well? Could you have done it better?

# H

## HELPLESS

*We do not want you to be unaware, brothers and sisters, of the affliction we experienced in Asia; for we were so utterly, unbearably crushed that we despaired of life itself.*

2nd Corinthians 1:8, NRSV

I HATE BEING helpless. Yet so often that seems to be the human condition. One gets on an airplane, buckles the seat belt, and waits to see what happens, having no control over events from take off to landing. It is the same with a train, or a bus, or an Uber, or a cab. Ann and I never felt so helpless as when our cab driver in Paris cut off a large truck.

    I recall standing watch with the Vietnamese in Danang at their Naval Command Center listening to a coastal installation up near the DMZ be overrun. We could hear the sounds of battle, carried on a hurried conversation with the Vietnamese at that station, and then there was silence. We were all in the same boat at the Command Center, totally helpless.

    So I have watched the evening news with video reports from the hospitals in New York and from New Orleans. I hear about the lack of masks and PPE for the nurses and physicians, or the dieticians and the janitorial staff, for everyone who is essential personnel.

    I hear my daughter in Los Angeles, counted as "essential personnel" as director of a health clinic, tell of driving across the city to fetch protective equipment for her clinic.

    And I am helpless. There is nothing I can do. It is out of my control.

    Grandchildren are at home; childcare can be an issue. But grandparents are helpless; there is no way to travel to get there to provide assistance. Friends, relatives die, for whatever reason; there is no way to have a service; families are helpless while loved ones die without them.

Security workers turn people away at hospital doors; they must do so to prevent transmission of the infection. They hear the pleas, and their inner voices say, "Oh, let them in!", but they are helpless.

Volunteers make masks. People experiment with new means of communication. Even in our 70's and 80's and 90's we are learning to Zoom and we practice by having Zoom Happy Hours. At least we are getting good at that. We struggle to find ways to make a meaningful contribution, to find some way to be helpful. I sit at my computer and type a script. I copy cartoons and jokes for the community bulletin boards. I help organize various video presentations. Yet still, in this crisis, I feel so helpless.

The future is uncertain. We do not know what the new "normal" will be. We wait and we feel helpless.

**Keywords:** waiting, silence, no way, uncertain, volunteers

When have you felt helpless? Has someone else made important decisions for you? When?

# I

## ISOLATED

*Jacob was left alone; and a man wrestled with him until daybreak.*
Genesis 32:24, NRSV

I WOKE UP in the recovery unit. It was November 7, 2001 and I had just had the leaky mitral valve in my heart replaced. A voice was prompting me, "Breathe! Breathe!" As I returned to semi-consciousness I was aware I was still intubated and that I was restrained so that I could not injure myself.

Though I knew I was being monitored and watched, I was terrified for I was totally at the mercy of someone else. However, it was better then the previous time I had been in isolation.

That had been at SERE (Survival, Evasion, Resistance & Escape) School in California before I went to Vietnam. It was on October 14, 1971, and I had, as my inner critic told me, done something really stupid and now I was hogtied, gagged, hoodwinked, and stuffed in a small metal box, isolated from all the other prisoners at the simulated POW camp where our group was being held.

I was being punished, in solitary confinement, isolated, left alone for several hours. At first I was angry and defiant, but as time passed I had to wrestle with the growing terror within me.

During this COVID pandemic we see many people alone in the hospital, isolated from those they love as they fight for their lives. Other around them are either gowned, masked, and wearing face shields or in a bed wrestling for life. I cannot imagine it is comforting.

Of the three experiences of isolation I have outlined, there is not one I would willingly choose. I found confinement and isolation terrible for this meant I was not in control of my own existence, but totally dependent upon others.

Even worse was being left alone to wrestle with my own thoughts and emotions, encouraged by that inner critic that thrives on such circumstances to put the worst possible spin on everything. I can remember being in that little box making an extensive mental list of everyone I would blame for my situation, starting with my local military recruiter.

But now we are expected, if we travel any distance from our community, to – upon our return – put ourselves in isolation for the sake of the larger community. After fourteen days pass, we are either freed, supposedly not able to transmit this dreaded infection, or confined elsewhere for we ourselves have developed the disease and are under treatment, hoping for the best. I can only imagine the inner conversation as one begins the fourteen-day isolation. Was whatever it was that brought us to this point – a move, a visit to an infected area, exposure to someone who had the disease – worth it?

**Keywords:** breathe, restrained, dependent, terror, wrestle

When was the last time you were involuntarily confined? Have you ever been caught in circumstances where there was no escape? What was the occasion?

# *J*

## JEALOUS

*As they were coming home, when David returned from killing the Philistine, the women came out of all the towns of Israel, singing and dancing, to meet King Saul, with tambourines, with songs of joy, and with musical instruments. And the women sang to one another as they made merry,*
    "*Saul has killed his thousands,*
        *and David his ten thousands.*"
*Saul was very angry, for this saying displeased him. He said, "They have ascribed to David ten thousands, and to me they have ascribed thousands; what more can he have but the kingdom?" So Saul eyed David from that day on.*

1<sup>st</sup> Samuel 18: 7-9, NRSV

DURING MY YEARS working in the church as a pastor and church executive, I had ample time to observe human nature at work. Certainly one of the most instructive times was when church budgets were being proposed and reviewed.

When the budgets were being assembled, committees gathered to formulate requests for new amounts. Displeased with the amount being received, some member would raise the manta, "Our work is worth as much as that other committee; look at their budget! We should ask for more money."

Committees were always evaluating the value of their work by how much was allocated to their task. Emotionally committee members were a bunch of Sauls thinking about how his numbers compared with David's.

During the review phase committees would invariably look at how much of their budgeted amount had been spent; if it was not all expended, some member would raise the mantra. "We need to spend it all or else we will have less next year."

Committee members were very jealous about protecting that which they already had and, if a surplus existed, feared that some other committee might attempt to steal those funds. Like Saul keeping his eye on David, it was time to protect the kingdom!

I do not believe that type of behavior – envy of a larger budget allocation and grasping on to what it already possessed – is unique to churches. It is simply part and parcel to human jealousy.

During this pandemic I can look out of my community and see people walking down to the waterfront, people riding bicycles and pushing carts, and neighbors gathering in yards to exchange news and have barbecues. They may, or may not, be masked and keeping social distance. I am envious. They are outside our locked down campus and I can see them and I want to do some of the things they are doing, but I cannot! We independent living residents are not leaving our campus or having visitors out of concern for the assisted living and Health Center residents. We do not want to be the ones that carry the COVID-19 into our facility. However, even though our confinement is voluntary, our human nature still has us looking enviously at those who are outside our gates enjoying a freedom of movement we have sacrificed.

Then, lest we here in our community appear too noble in sacrificing that freedom to come and go and to have visitors, I should also note that we recognize that we, as senior citizens, are all part of the "vulnerable" segment and we want to protect our own health.

Our inner critics, the little nagging voices, are having fun with our jealousy.

**Keywords:** evaluating, value, guard, envious, sacrificed

Is the grass greener next door? Does your neighbor have a newer computer? More grandchildren?

# *K*

## KNOWING

*The mind of one who has understanding seeks knowledge,*
*but the mouths of fools feed on folly.*
Proverbs 15:14, NRSV

YOU ARE OBVIOUSLY someone seeking knowledge. You are watching this video on YouTube. How you found this presentation I do not know. Perhaps a friend who thought you might be interested shared it with you. Or perhaps you typed in some search word – pandemic – and this was among the great variety of offering that appeared. Or perhaps YouTube, using some mysterious algorithms, chose this video for you based upon your previous viewing history.

If nothing else, this pandemic has forced us – the senior citizens – into the new age of electronic and digital communication. We hold our meetings and Happy Hours by Zoom. We communicate with family on Facebook, Twitter and Instagram. We visit using Skype or Facetime. We pay bills online, order our groceries and medications, and fill our needs through online shopping APPs. We still use the old fashioned email for some communications. I hope you realize I am describing what a group of senior citizens are doing; we are not yet conversant with any newer APPs, but we are learning.

However, the downside to this is that we are all getting much of our information through electronic medium of one kind or another as, during this pandemic, newspapers and magazines have switched to online versions. With the lockdown, we are, of course, curious about what is happening. The various platforms on our computer, the search engines, are only too glad to provide us with all sorts of information, labeling this activity as a civic responsibility, while in truth they all are using the time we spend to sell access time to various advertisers of dubious worth.

We are already inundated with political and special interest advertisements. All this comes to us pretty much unfiltered. We can, of course, choose between Fox news and MSNBC, but if we follow them online, then that information is monetized by Google, Yahoo and the others as they sell more viewing time based upon the channels we access so that similar channels can have access to what is left of our minds. Our poor minds can only hold so much, especially when what we receive is so damn in tune with what we feel. This distracting digital monster has succeeded in blurring feelings, emotions and knowledge having any factual base. To maintain my sanity, I only consult email and Facebook in the morning and evening, and I turn off the television and radio for extended periods during the day. It is too easy to get hooked by some tweet or talking head or passing post, and say, "That's great; I have to share it!" My inner critic, knowing I have been emotionally hooked, says, "Do it!" So I do, without any consideration for the truth of the "share" or of the effect this "share" might have on others.

I want to understand, so I do seek knowledge based on fact not emotional appeal; but I rarely find this online and do not want to spend time trying to pick it our of all the posts and "shares." Online APPs provide the "mouth of fools" opportunities to proffer "folly." This is not the sustaining wisdom or knowledge I seek.

**Keywords:** new age, electronic medium, inundated, digital monster, hooked

Is there a source of knowledge you trust? What is it? Who is it?

# *L*

## LABELED

*As Jesus was walking along, he saw a man called Matthew sitting at the tax booth, and he said to him, "Follow me." And he got up and followed him. And as he sat at dinner in the house, many tax collectors and sinners came and were sitting with him and his disciples. When the Pharisees saw this, they said, to his disciples, "Why does your teacher eat with tax collectors and sinners?"*

Matthew 9:9-11, NRSV

FATHER, GRANDFATHER, pastor, and veteran: these are some of the words I use when I willingly label myself if asked who I am. Labels allow us to easily and conveniently associate with a larger similar group and can be modified to provide more specific information, for example: *College graduate, Syracuse, English, 1968, Acacia Fraternity.*

During this 2020 census we are asked to identify certain labels that apply to us so that resources and representation may be apportioned as equitably as possible. We recognize that this use of labels is appropriate and useful; the labels themselves are simply tools to a greater end; and, since we have chosen our own labels, they are emotionally neutral.

However, labels we apply to others are not neutral for they are burdened by assumptions that may or may not be appropriate. Who has not, driving through sections of a large city, looked out the window in a run down neighborhood and asked if the car doors were locked? We have labeled that neighborhood unsafe and have taken action. That label may not necessarily be appropriate for that neighborhood, but, nevertheless, we have applied it and acted upon it.

In same vein, recently during the Minneapolis unrest, a major network reporter, a Black/Hispanic man, was arrested while another nearby reporter from the same network, white, was not. Both were wearing similar identification at the same time. The arresting officers made assumptions – dangerous or not dangerous – about the reporters based on their appearance, and, as is so often the case, the assumption, the label, was wrong.

During this pandemic we have seen labels misapplied. Since the virus was first labeled the "corona" virus, people began to boycott the Mexican beer **Corona** and Hispanic people were ostracized. Then it became the "China Flu" and Chinese communities around the nation became targets for those who would assign a label – inappropriately – and, acting on nothing but emotion, violently attack businesses and individuals.

In our own communities we are apt to assign labels easily and make decisions based upon our emotional labeling. Someone without a mask is one who "does not care" about others. Someone is seen returning to the community by car and is now a "threat to us all." Since we already know we are the "vulnerable elderly" or, as a couple living together, a "germ sharing unit," it follows that we are tempted by our inner critic to assign ourselves labels thinking that we are "victims" or "helpless." The emotional toll exacted by the pandemic may eventually reveal us as victims, but perhaps not. If we confront the labels we apply and the emotions those labels evoke honestly and often during the pandemic, we may avoid some of the emotional turmoil that is yet to occur.

**Keywords:** useful, assumptions, misapplied, emotional labeling, yet to occur

Have you have ever been wrongly labeled? How did that feel? Did it affect your life in some way? How? Have you labeled people and discovered your label was wrong?

# *M*

## MANIPULATED

*In the morning David wrote a letter to Joab and sent it by the hand of Uriah. In the letter he wrote, "Set Uriah in the forefront of the hardest fighting, and then draw back from him, so that he may be struck down and die."*
2nd Samuel 11:14,15, NRSV

BEING AMBUSHED is terrifying. Setting and carrying out an ambush is an exercise in strict control of assets and can be strangely satisfying. But every ambush exacts a price. Here King David sets an ambush, not to win a battle, but to steal a woman with whom he has had an affair and impregnated, Uriah's wife. The ambush is successful; Uriah dies and David marries Bathsheba. However, the child, not long after birth, dies.

An ambush is the ultimate form of manipulation, but it sets the pattern for any manipulative activity. To be the victim of manipulation, when one realizes it, is a humbling, heart-breaking experience for an ambush is meant to profit off the victim. The one who initiates a manipulation, if successful, is satisfied for that person gains something desired, be it information or wealth or power. However, eventually the master manipulator will pay a price.

It is one thing, the "old game," to manipulate for information or wealth or power. It is quite another level of manipulation when one uses as an asset something one cannot control, like a plague.

During this pandemic there has been a lot of manipulation. From the outset of the pandemic, facts and numbers were being manipulated and hidden and denied. Expectations were raised, proved untrue, and then denied.

The history of this COVID-19 pandemic will not please those who have been in control of the manipulation; they will pay a price. But that is all in the future.

Right now we are in the struggle to keep from falling into the various, changing ambushes the manipulators are setting, for having failed to succeed early, they continue to attempt to salvage something, to win, for that is the goal of an ambush.

Those who have been taken in, though humbled, still can be a part of frustrating the ongoing manipulation. Those who have fallen victim to the failed manipulation of the uncontrollable "asset" – COVID-19 – can have some satisfaction by setting aside their sorrow, anger, and loss to share stories of their experiences. Those who have not been seduced, by good fortune or attending to the warnings about the manipulation, must be determined to continue to seek for and insist on accurate information and true accountability.

When I spoke about fear I outlined responses based upon the pattern of human emotions when ambushed: panic, fear, and action. One was the warrior response of attacking those bringing the ambush. Another was the shepherd response of forming a committee to discern a response. A third response, grounded in fear, was hoping that by some magic miracle, the infection would go away or just disappear. The last, which I preferred, was to recognize the problem, react appropriately based on the best and most accurate information, adopt temporary measures buying time to develop treatment protocols and perhaps a vaccine, and then, with determination, set a goal of establishing a new "normal" that informs our preparations for the next pandemic.

My inner critic says, "You fool." To which I respond, "I am not a fool. I know that ambush trail. The fool is the one who will not act in hope."

**Keywords:** pattern, asset, ambush, humbling, facts and numbers, fool, warning

When was the last time someone took advantage of you? And you of someone else? Did either time really feel good? Why?

# N

## NERVOUS

*So do not worry about tomorrow, for tomorrow will bring worries of its own. Today's trouble is enough for today.*

Matthew 6:34, NRSV

I HAVE A PHLEGMATIC personality, as did my father, so trying to speak of anxiety or nervousness may seem to be a challenge. However, I have close family members who have more of a "Calamity Jane" personality so I am not unaccustomed to seeing molehills become mountains. I saw much of the same in the various churches I have served and quickly learned not to dismiss or discount someone's anxiety. Rather, believing as I do, that emotions are neither right nor wrong, they just are, I would listen carefully in order to validate the reality of the emotion and then explore with the individual what might be a possible creative response. If the person were interested I indicated I would be willing to talk with them to help them better understand why they became anxious in certain situations.

Having said that I will admit to some anxiety just before I would go on stage in a play, but that quickly dissipated as soon as the actual play began. During this pandemic I have heard a number of expressions of anxiety that are well founded. People around me are anxious about their possible exposure to COVID-19; after all we are a community of senior citizens and many of us have underlying health issues that make us even more vulnerable. We have a right to be anxious, to wear masks, wash hands, and maintain six feet of separation.

There is anxiety about children and grandchildren and their futures. Couple that with feelings of helplessness to do anything about cancelled graduations, uncertainty about education, and listening to the lamentations of parents who fear there will be no summer jobs for their offspring and you can begin to understand why our recycling barrels are full of wine and beer bottles as well as increasing whiskey and gin bottles.

This pandemic has caused the stock market to fluctuate a good deal. This is not comforting to retired people who are depending upon investments to maintain their lifestyle. We are also of an age that remembers the horrors of the nursing home industry of the last century. No one really wants to go back there. So there is much anxiety about ability to continue to pay fees and bills even though in our community there is a fund to assist those who run short, through no fault of their own, of funds to pay fees.

With the general anxiety of our nation, a feeling of dis-ease that is being fed by turmoil at all levels of government, the general deterioration of respect for institutions trusted in the past – police, churches, court, legislatures, executives – as such institutions and individuals are seen to be more concerned with survival then with service, it is no wonder the level of anxiety increases as fast as the case load and death toll of COVID-19.

Our interior critics prod and poke us, saying "What about tomorrow?" And it hard to say, "Right now we are doing fine."

**Keywords:** molehills and mountains, well founded, futures, fluctuate, dis-ease, deterioration

Are we doing fine right now? Why? Or why not?

# O

## OVERWHELMED

*Fear and trembling come upon me, and horror overwhelms me. And I say, "O that I had wings like a dove! I would fly away and be at rest..."*
                                                    Psalm 55:5,6, NRSV

"WE DON'T KNOW where we are!" This is what a resident in his nineties said to me. He and his wife, faced with multiple health problems, had to move from independent living into assisted living recently. Because of the current COVID-19 crisis, the ban from having any visitor come onto our campus, and the sheer difficulty of travel, the family, working through the administration, had to arrange for a local moving company (one trusted by and well-known to our community) to do the physical moving. Some items had to go into storage; others into the new apartment. There were various steps that had to be taken when moving out of one unit into another, from one status into another. Even though the administration acted with compassion, accompanying the couple, and patiently explaining over and over what was happening and why, the couple was just completely overwhelmed. "I wish we were somewhere else!" he said.

This is what it is like to be overwhelmed by events in a senior living facility. It is not uncommon, and the community moves to be supportive in such situations. Hopefully the family will be able to visit soon and the couple will begin to adjust to their new status.

But for those who have been heavily involved, and still are involved in the pandemic crisis – medical workers of all sorts, caregivers in a variety of senior care facilities, dieticians, custodial stuff, the list goes on – the reality of being overwhelmed is the new "normal."

And it is not only those on the front line. Spare a moment to think of the families of all those workers – parents who have not been home for weeks, fearful of carrying the infection into their homes, couples who have not seen each other for weeks, fearful of infecting each other, and this list goes on.

The Psalmist's description of being overwhelmed is disturbingly accurate. In the healing retreats I helped lead with veterans and partners a participant used a term to describe what being overwhelmed was like – "It was a flood! I was just completely swept away by emotions and I could not control anything, not even what I was doing. I was being tossed and turned so much I didn't know which way was up!"

During the Vietnam era, some news organization began publishing weekly lists with pictures of the warriors killed in that war. In later conflicts, in Iraq, Afghanistan, PBS NewsHour ended its nightly broadcast showing pictures of our nation's men and women killed in these wars. Now the PBS NewsHour is weekly remembering just some of the over 100,000 American citizens lost during the current pandemic – in five months almost twice the number lost in the Vietnam War. To show all the pictures of the COVID-19 victims nightly would leave no time for any other news.

No wonder we want to be somewhere else.

**Keywords:** not uncommon, front line, flood, tossed and turned, somewhere else

What kinds of events have you experienced that left you overwhelmed? How did that affect you?

# P

## PRESENCE

*Even though I walk through the darkest valley, I fear no evil; for you are with me; your rod and your staff – they comfort me.*

Psalm 23:4, NRSV

"SURELY THE PRESENCE of the Lord is in this place. I can feel God's mighty power and God's grace."[2] I love to begin worship services with this song for it gives permission to the gathered people to let down their emotional guard and allow themselves to be aware of the mystery that there exists a presence both outside and within them. Often in Vietnam warriors would say that God was AWOL.[3] I never felt that way. Even in the worst of moments – when I was holding a dying man – I was aware that neither he nor I was alone. I put it this way: "I didn't have time to either feel or cry, so Jesus did it for me."

We have seen the videos of hospitals around the world overwhelmed by this pandemic: not enough beds, not enough ventilators, not enough people, not enough of anything. We see pictures of body bags and caskets lined up. We hear that funeral homes are literally stuffed with dead bodies waiting to be buried or cremated, but there are not enough caskets available, or workers to open graves, or working crematoriums. So the dead wait. Surely this is a vision of hell on earth.

Families cannot gather at a bedside to hold the hand of the dying or give a final kiss or hug. They cannot even gather at the funeral home or the church or at the grave.

---

[2] "Surely the Presence of the Lord" ©1977 by Lanny Wolfe Music. All rights controlled by Gaither Copyright Management.

[3] AWOL means 'absent without leave."

Who is present when the last breath is drawn, or the remains are rolled in the crematorium retort or lowered into the earth?

Presbyterian minster Fred Rogers, best know for his children's program **Mr. Roger's Neighborhood**, once said, "When I was a boy and I would see scary things in the news, my mother would say to me, 'Look for the helpers. You will always find people who are helping.'" During this pandemic that is good advice. For even in the great loneliness we see in the hospitals and the emptiness we feel when we cannot be with a loved one to offer comfort or say good-by, we recognize that there are courageous helpers doing their best. We can look past our absence to see their presence.

It is not only in the hospitals that we find the presence of helpers. Grocery stores, drugstores, gas stations, truck stops, essential places that we depend upon to fill our orders and deliver those items are staffed by men and women who are helpers, though perhaps they never thought of themselves in that way; nor did we, until now.

Those words that I love to use in worship are now, I can see, appropriate words when I enter any facility and look at the people working there as more than employees, but as helpers. Perhaps this change in my attitude, my way of observing people, will make a difference in my life, making it a bit more joyful during hard times; I hope so. Perhaps it will even make a difference in the lives of the people I encounter in the aisle or at the cash register or at the service counter. Who knows? For them, even my presence may open some door, and do some good.

**Keywords:** mystery, hell on earth, who is present, helpers, do some good

Has someone showing up been a positive experience for you? When did that happen? Have you shown up unexpectedly to help someone? How did that feel?

# Q

## QUEASY

*My inward parts are in turmoil, and are never still; days of affliction come to meet me. I go about in sunless gloom; I stand up in the assembly and cry for help.*
Job 30:27,28, NRSV

I LIVE IN FLORIDA so it is difficult to talk about sunless gloom. We just talk about the gloominess brought about by this pandemic. We cannot even stand up in "the assembly" and complain; we are more likely to do that then "cry for help." That does not mean that our "inward parts" are not in turmoil, for they are, and it is not from something we ate or drank.

I think each of us is aware that there is some situation that will cause us to become queasy, ill at ease in our "inward parts." Perhaps it's waiting at the dentist's office, or maybe at the airport, or sitting on the plane waiting for takeoff. I know of a multitude of competent, confident people whose insides turned to jelly if I had managed to coerce them into being a liturgist at a Sunday worship service. Just the idea of public speaking sends many people searching for the nearest restroom. And not only are we aware of that sensitive point, so is our inner critic who delights in reminding us about that "weakness." The voice says, "Oh, you know you can't do that! Think of how your stomach will feel." And, then, even if we are not committed to do whatever it is that makes us queasy, just a reminder from our inner critic suffices to bring up that emotion!

One discussion topic I have found will pretty much make everyone queasy. No one wants to talk about death! Just try starting a conversation with "What's going to happen to this antique when you die?" or "Let's talk about your funeral arrangements." or "Do you want to be intubated in the hospital?" Generally that will either end the conversation or produce a rapid change of subject.

I try to sneak it into a conversation surreptitiously. "What did you think about the funeral service for Aunt Emma?" or "Have you heard of the 'grave adopters' at the American Cemetery in the Netherlands?" As soon as the hearers become aware that the real topic is going to be planning for their death and funeral arrangements, they begin to turn green and shift about as their "inward parts" begin to rumble and tumble.

COVID-19 is not making anything easier. People are being struck down never having even broached the topic of "intubation" or "extraordinary measures." A loved one dies and there are absolutely no instructions they have left; often not even a will can be found.

Talk about being caught in emotional turmoil? Here it comes! "How could he (or she) do this to me? Die? And leave me not knowing where the checkbook is! Or the insurance policies! Or anything!" "I don't even know if he had a will!" Anger at the deceased for having died is not unusual. Emotions, some justified and some not, of abandonment, betrayal, and rage will mix with grief, loneliness, and helplessness. Often, all the emotions are so overwhelming that numbness sets in and everyone is frozen in place, unable to make any decisions.

And then the "inward parts" tumble as those left behind think about property deeds, estates, and lawyers. Talk about feeling queasy!

No one thinks they are going to die or be struck down in the next twenty-four hours. But it will happen for we all have a final twenty-four hours; we just to do not know when the clock begins ticking.

**Keywords:** "inward parts," jelly, death, turmoil, numbness, twenty-four hours

Have you made your will? Reviewed it? How about a living will?

# R

## RESTLESS

*Among the nations you will find no ease, no resting place for the sole of your foot. There the Lord will give you a trembling heart, failing eyes, and a languishing spirit. Your life shall hang in doubt before you; night and day you shall be in dread, with no assurance of your life. In the morning you shall say, "If only it were evening!" and at the evening you shall say, "if only it were morning!" — because of the dread your heart shall feel and the sights that your eyes shall see.*

Deuteronomy 28:65-67, NRSV

I LIKE TO BE ON TIME. In fact, I prefer to get places a bit early. If I have a doctor's appointment or am officiating at some sort of service, I will always get there well ahead of time. However, I have tried to apply my philosophy to events such as going to the theater or to a dinner engagement. This has caused some discussion between my wife and me. I have been bluntly told that arriving for a dinner party fifteen minutes before the appointed time is not necessarily a good idea! I have had to accept this truth, but even accepting this reality does not stop me from getting ready early and restlessly pacing back and forth looking at the clock, thereby irritating my wife. Meanwhile, my inner critic is whispering, "You're going to be late! You should have already left! You'll get caught in traffic!"

The curse of restlessness is pretty well described in the passage above. No matter how completely we have made arrangement for a trip, I don't sleep well the night before we travel. I want to get going.

In this pandemic period, we are being advised, "Stay at home." This does not sit well with us for we retired to a CCR so we could travel and not worry about a piece of property.

We have a time-share, travel points accumulated, our set aside funds for the adventures of our senior years and we can't take advantage of any of it. We feel like caged animals.

Now our situation and these feelings may seem like small potatoes; but emotions are neither right nor wrong, they just are. What matters is that we recognize and honor these emotions and evaluate their appropriateness and then choose how we will respond.

So we acknowledge that we are disappointed that planned reunions have been cancelled, weddings have taken place and that possible receptions may happen in the future, that some fun times with friends and family have had to be delayed and that we are living in the this time when we cannot even begin to make any plans because the COVID-19 pandemic may only be in the opening round. However, we also realize that much of this is beyond our control and that we do not have many options. But we do have some.

So we choose to use Facetime and Zoom to communicate. We do our best to keep lines of sharing open using a variety of media. And we choose to look ahead, making plans with no firm dates for implementation, but allowing ourselves the pleasure of planning and anticipation. We also have started more walking to burn off energy and our pool has reopened so we can use that as well. After all, we want to be in shape when we are able to travel freely. So we choose to be optimistic about the future. But I still pace around restlessly. But that's all right; it is part of who I am.

**Keywords:** get going, caged animals, disappointed, beyond control, choose

How do you handle restless moments? When do they hit? Do you see choices you have? What are they?

# S

## SADNESS

*For in much wisdom is much vexation, and those who increase knowledge increase sorrow.*

Ecclesiastes 1:18, NRSV

DEEP SADNESS AND GRIEF are the most difficult emotions I have to confront. Part of this is because I accepted a call to serve my country and went to war. During the course of my tour of duty I had to kill. I did so, but doing it violated my belief system, shattering the boundaries of my faith. I survived when others did not. My inner critic has been my cruelest and most constant companion over these years, driving me into self-destructive behaviors. It took a long time to confront the emotions of the losses I inflicted and bore, as I feared the deep emotion of sadness. With help, I confronted that pain and started the slow, painful journey to peace.

The reality is that the longer we live, the more we have to grieve. Parents, relatives, children, friends, admired mentors, and others seem to pass from our presence; we miss their voices, laughter, and loving touch. Sometimes memories and that inner voice vex us saying, "You should have spent more time with them" or "You could have remembered her birthday." I resolutely choose to beat down that voice by reminding myself how grateful I am for the presence in my life of those I have lost.

When the cost of this pandemic period is totaled, the greatest price will be the one paid by the families of those who have died, some because neither treatment nor equipment was available; the one paid by the caregivers who survived who wish they could have done more; and the one paid by the minorities who were the victims of xenophobic and racist attacks.

However, each of us will also have paid a substantial price for we have been witnesses to the growing toll taken by the pandemic as well as to the manner in which the pandemic has been politicized and monetized by irresponsible leadership which sought personal gain and power over national wellbeing. And we will have been witnesses to the power of xenophobia and racism to destroy the lives and livelihoods of the innocent.

Many will have paid a personal price in the loss of a someone beloved and then finding themselves unable to console the grieving left behind or share with them the human touch of comfort and care.

We pray that a vaccine will be created and that effective treatment protocols will be developed so that others may not know the deep grief of loss to the ravages of this disease. But this will not take away the deep sadness, for as we know more about this disease, about how our national leaders responded or did not respond, our sorrow will only increase.

And yes, tears will flow, or try to flow. Crying is not an attractive activity. No one looks their best with tears streaming, loudly sobbing, shoulders shaking. Yet, if you feel like crying, please do. If you try and stuff your tears away, you will end up denying the sadness and all the other the emotions that are causing the tears. I have used an image with veterans that put them a bit more at ease with tears. This example seems to validate the usefulness of crying. I tell them, "When a weapon get stuck, we have to grease it to get it to work. Just so, tears are the grease for the spirit that will get you moving to the next step. Do not be ashamed of them, but value them for what they are."

**Keywords:** violated, grieve, price, did not respond, sorrow increase, tears, grease

What makes you cry? Why? What was lost?

## TEMPTED

*But the serpent said to the woman, "You will not die; for God knows when you eat of it [the fruit] your eyes will be opened, and you will be like God, knowing good and evil." . . . she took of its fruit and ate; and she also gave some to her husband, who was with her, and he ate. Then their eyes were opened, and they knew they were naked.*

Genesis 3:4-7, NRSV

OUR INNER CRITIC enjoys tempting us. "That extra slice of pie won't hurt you!" "Go ahead – have another beer!" "So you forgot your mask. You're only going to Walgreens!"

And so the inner voice tempts us, and once more we give in.

It looks so tempting to go out for a walk, and now the beaches are open again. "No one will be up at the lake right now; we can slip up there and put the dock in." And so we do and then that inner voice says, "You what? You were so thoughtless that now you have probably carried that COVID back here with you!"

Human beings have been giving in to temptation with a "What the hell – it can't hurt you!" attitude since the earliest stories were told around the campfires of the traveling merchants. Many of the best traveling salesman stories involve giving in to some temptation. All great literature exists because someone gave in to some temptation: to seize power, to have a forbidden love, to want what someone else has, to be in control like a god. Without temptation, there would be no Shakespeare or, for that matter, no musical comedy.

Yet there is certainly one temptation it is worthwhile to resist: the human tendency to devalue oneself, to give in to the idea that your life has no meaning or purpose. This practice of self-rejection is insidious and one of the favorite of my inner voice. "You never could do anything right!" it whispers as I hit the nail and it bends.

As we see the pandemic's mounting death toll around the world rise, its sheer magnitude tempts us to shut the whole business out. There was a saying during the Vietnam War: "It don't mean nothing." It referred to a belief that, when all was said and done, a life that was lost – your own or someone else's – really didn't matter. No one was even bothering to keep score. It becomes easy to say his or her life didn't matter as long as you believe that your own life is inconsequential as well. It was a real temptation and many fell into it, got careless, and died thinking no one cared. But that was not true; the 58,000 plus names on **The Wall**[4] testify to the reality that someone did care, someone still cares.

In the face of mounting numbers and with great pain, we still insist that every life matters, including our own. We cannot reject the importance of their lives without rejecting our own. The patient struggling to live is God's beloved child. The nurse by the bedside is God's beloved child. The weeping mother is God's beloved child. To affirm them, and the reality of their loss, is to affirm our own place as God's beloved child.

**Keywords:** give in, can't hurt you, devalue, didn't matter, beloved child

What tempts you? What does that say about you? Do you define yourself by the temptations to which you have succumbed?

---

[4] The Vietnam National Memorial

# U

## UNKNOWN

*Did I not weep for those whose day was hard? Was not my soul grieved for the poor? But when I looked for good, evil came; and when I waited for light, darkness came.*

Job 30:25,26, NRSV

THE GREATEST FEAR we have is the unknown, but then the unknown of the next moment is one of the few certainties of life. As a church executive I could have a full day of committee meetings scheduled with prepared agendas, with goals in sight, and then at the first meeting a committee member might arrive who had just learned of a family member's death. The entire agenda for that meeting would change as committee members offered various kinds of support and comfort. The people at the second meeting, having heard of the first, would be distracted, and so the day would go on. It never upset me – the business would still be there and most of it could wait – because I always believed that people and their lives came before the business of an organization. And besides, such events always encouraged me for I had the opportunity to see how good and caring and tender people could be.

I have never really liked Job; he didn't need an inner critic because he was one, always claiming to have done the best for all and then constantly complaining that no one appreciated him, or that he was unjustly persecuted. So he anticipated that things would go badly. His attitude and experience sums up the experience of those who fear the unknown. They see the evil or the darkness and take no further risk. They sit down and complain rather then confront the evil and walk into the darkness.

My experience has been different. I embrace the unknown. I am grateful for the unknown for it affirms that there is still a lot to be discovered, that there is something new around the next bend or over the next hill. For me, stepping out into an uncertain future is the great adventure that makes life worth living. Job and his ilk prefer to sit on their ashes and complain.

There is no doubt that this COVID-19 is evil in the sense that it is destructive; this is how I define evil: it destroys the chance for future creation. But for those who are confronting the evil, taking the risk, looking for the treatment protocol, in bravely taking action they affirm that risking the unknown is worth it for it is only when we step out that a treatment will be found, that a vaccine may be possible. And the experience of history is that the risk is always worth it, though the price maybe great.

Now people may argue with me saying that no one in their right mind would take such risks willingly. To which I would respond, "You are wrong. Every member of the Armed Forces takes an oath that they will step out and risk dying so you can have the choice to sit on an ash heap or to take your own risky step into some unknown future."

That is why I love military parade music. Some hate it because they say the music is inspiring young men and women to march off to kill and die. I say it is young men and women stepping into the unknown, setting an example of what it means to take a risk for a bright future.

**Keywords:** certainties, sit on ashes, step out, risk, future

Do you know what is going to happen in an hour? Two hours? Tomorrow? Next week? Would you want to know?

# V

## VULNERABLE

*My God, my God, why have you forsaken me? Why are you so far from helping me, from the words of my groaning? O my God, I cry by day, but you do not answer; and by night, but find no rest.*

Psalm 22:1,2, NRSV

THESE ARE THE WORDS of human uncertainty, of abject loneliness, of helplessness. Such terrifying, fearful thoughts afflicted Jesus hanging on the cross so he fell back on the words of the Psalmist. Many vulnerable people over the decades have depended upon the Psalms for words to validate the reality – sometimes good, sometimes bad – that they are currently experiencing. I memorized several Psalms to recite during trying times in Vietnam, and, though I never recall reciting an entire Psalm, that were certainly phrases that popped into my mind at various odd times.

Throughout this COVID-19 crisis we have had many images of frightened, lonely, anxious people – often only being able to see their eyes. One wonders if these eyes tell stories of fear, or abandonment, or loneliness, or hopelessness. Certainly the eyes reflect the vulnerability of one facing an uncertain future.

I have sometimes offered what I have called my pandemic blessing: "When you meet a person with a mask, may you see the eyes of God's beloved child; when you wash your hands, may you see the hands of God's beloved servant; and when you maintain that six feet of separation, may you bridge that space with a mutual blessing, one both given and received, wishing good health to the one you meet upon the trail, always looking for the gift that person brings to your life."

I offer this blessing to emphasize that God's presence can be as near as the closest helping person. However, the Psalmist reflects the feelings of the vulnerable person who perceives God as being at a great distance, almost inaccessible. This gap, this space, is what I refer to in my benediction as the one that we need to bridge with a mutual blessing, as we try to discern a gift in that relationship.

Admittedly, it is much harder to see a gift when God seems to be far away, or even absent. I do not know what that gift might be. Perhaps it comes with a growing awareness of something being lost or something being gained, as if one is disappearing or being welcomed into a bright, warm light. I simply do not know.

I do know that this seeming difference in the perception of God as either being far away or close by has been a constant theme of faith discussions over the centuries. I also know that this vulnerability is felt and shared by my inner critic because in this discussion, no inner voice speaks. There is only a silence; and perhaps this is the gift the bridges the space between God at a distance and God close by.

**Keywords:** loneliness, closest helper, distance, perception, gift, silence

For you, is there a creative presence near by or one at a distance? Have you felt abandoned or betrayed? When? How does that affect you?

# W

## WISTFUL

*By the rivers of Babylon – there we say down and wept when we remembered Zion. On the willows there we hung up our harps. For there our captors asked us for songs, and our tormentors asked for mirth, saying, "Sing us one of the songs of Zion!" How could we sing the Lord's song in a foreign land?*

Psalm 137:1-4, NRSV

"AH, YES, I REMEMBER IT WELL." goes the song from the 1958 musical *Gigi*.[5] These are words of the refrain as Honore attempts to recall a date with Mamita. Unfortunately he is wrong in every detail, but he wistfully sings his refrain, "Ah, yes, I remember it well." There is something entrancingly lovely about what once was, but what is no more.

You can hear that wistfulness in the words of the 137th Psalm. "If we could only go back to Zion, all would be as it was." No one is immune to the siren call of nostalgia. Even my inner critic longs for the "good old days," regularly reminding me that I should be able to do as many push ups as I did when I was twenty-five.

Feeling nostalgic, in 2014, I took my wife to Monterey, CA, where I had been stationed back in 1970, prior to moving to the Defense Language School in Monterey to study North Vietnamese. The occasion was a dinner being held at the Naval Postgraduate School to celebrate the anniversary of the Language School. As a disabled veteran I was able to get a room at in the main building of the Post Graduate School, an old hotel. I drove up to the front door and was greeted like a senior officer, a big change from my 1970 enlisted experience when I was not allowed to use the front door!

Right now there is a lot of nostalgia for the pre-COVID-19 days when we could go to restaurants, the beach, and theaters. Living

---

[5] 1958 Broadway musical written by Alan Jay Learner and Frederick Lowe.

in a senior community, many of us relish times when we can say "Remember when . . . ." and then launch into a story of times fifty years ago.

What is it that we cherish from the past? Well, there did not seem to be as much uproar. But most of all, we knew where we stood in relationship to the people around us. The heady years of marriage, children, family get-togethers and trips were hallmarks of the "good life." There was a sense of security, stability, and inevitability when we said "Good-by! See you next year!" Now, thanks to COVID-19, we have no idea when, and if, we will ever see some of our family and friends again.

There was even a rhythm to sickness. Spring colds, allergies, summer sniffles, fall allergies, and then flu in the winter. But now unexpected reports of new breakouts and "hot spots" preclude traveling. Rumors and threats of a second round, more deadly then the first, have everyone being very cautious.

We want the good old days back, but we are not going to get them. Instead we must summon our determination and go forward into a new time, when even our native land may feel like a "foreign country."

**Keywords:** nostalgia, remember, security, inevitability, rhythm, good old days, "foreign country"

How have you changed over the years? Have you told your story to anyone? Written it down? What do you miss the most?

# X

## XENOPHOBIA

*A man was going down from Jerusalem to Jericho, and fell into the hands of robbers, who stripped him, beat him, and went away leaving him half dead . . . a priest was going by . . . and passed by on the other side . . . so likewise a Levite . . . But a Samaritan while traveling came near him, and when he saw him, he was moved with pity.*

Luke 10:30-33, NRSV

THE WORD OF THE DAY: xenophobia – fear or hatred of foreigners, people from different cultures, or strangers. While it is true that COVID-19 does not target any national group, it is also true that certain groups seem to be more susceptible to becoming the victims of this disease.

I recall the original lists included people living and working in senior care facilities, especially Extended Care units, and senior citizens with complicating health issues. Since then other hot spots have been identified such as prisons and meat packing plants. Because of the dynamics of incarceration practices and employment in these industries, they appear to incubators for transmission of the pandemic.

Also, it has become evident that COVID-19 is claiming more victims among people of color than among white people. It has become apparent, as well, that the lower income workers who are easily overlooked and are now the "essential workers" keeping the health care system functioning are disproportionately becoming COVID victims.

Now this news is unpleasant enough for minority groups, but add the depressing reality that both Mexicans and Chinese minorities and businesses have been targeted: the former because of a ridiculous myth involving coronavirus and Corona beer and the latter because of an insistence by our nation's leader in labeling coronavirus the "China flu." Such labeling certainly has stoked our current national slide into a toxic mix of xenophobia and resurgent racism.

As I am writing this, the pandemic has claimed more the 100,000 victims, but the nation's attention is focused on the death of one black man at the hands of white Minneapolis policemen. As I am writing this protestors are filling the streets in Minneapolis-St Paul as well as New York, Los Angeles, Atlanta, Washington, D.C., and other cities. It is similar to the long nights of the 1960's.

Certainly as this pandemic is discussed, as the after-effects on our society are evaluated, the resurgence of xenophobia and racism will be an important part of the conversation. The hopeful sign, if there is any, is that the protestors are more diverse than were the crowds of the sixties.

For those of us who recall the violence of the sixties, the levels of hatred expressed for minorities, the complicity of various levels of leadership, this is an emotional blow revealing the weakness of the façade of the equality we had worked to build. How could it all fall apart so quickly?

**Keywords:** fear, different cultures, racism, violence, façade, victims

Were you taught to distrust certain people? What was the distrust based on? Has your view of people from different cultures and countries evolved? In what manner?

# *Y*

## YEARNING

*For I am longing to see you so that I may share with you some spiritual gift to strengthen you – or rather so that we may be mutually encouraged by each other's faith, both yours and mine.*
Romans 1:11, NRSV

STAY AT HOME ORDERS in our community have been in force for three months now. We are all doing pretty well. We in independent living can leave the campus, but must run the gauntlet at the gate to get back in, having our temperatures taken and recorded, accounting for where have been and why, who we've seen, and how long we've been gone. If we break the rules, we are expected to self-quarantine for 14 days. I have left for blood tests at the VA[6] Hospital, to make a rare trip to the grocery store or drugstore, and twice to go to local distilleries where I can call in an order and they bring the liquor out to my car.

    Though restrictions in our state of Florida are beginning to loosen up a bit, we are still being very careful hoping the number of new cases will decrease. However, accurate information is hard to come by as the state government, in thrall to the example set by national leadership, is playing games and cooking the figures to make things look better then they are. There is no trustworthy information coming from the higher levels of government so we have to count on local officials and news sources for any kind of believable information.

    We long for a return to some sort of a schedule of activities in our community, enough so that we could reliably tell what day it is! And for our dining room to open up in some form so we can sit with

---

[6] Veterans Administration

the other residents and tell stories about how we all spent the last three or months, stories of all the things we did not do.

We yearn for the freedom to travel around our area without having to account for our every move. I know I want to pick up again with the young people at the Improv Theatre where I had been taking classes, but I have to balance that desire with the need to take precautions until a reliable vaccine is created. I certainly do not want to be the one who brings the virus onto out campus.

We know that we will have to learn some new habits. I think we all have the cleanest hands we have ever had. People are getting more adept at sneezing into their elbows, though some of the contortions to do so are amusing. Social distancing and masks may be around for while, but eventually the masks will disappear and we will once more be able to hug.

And as time passes, more and more people will begin to wonder why they can't sleep at night. They will feel strange about not being able to go into a store or into a theater and inquire why one of them insists on sitting far to the front of the church where no one ever goes. The sight of a large group together will make them nervous and they will ask, "What's wrong with me? Why can't I have the good old days back when nothing bothered me?" And the answer will be, "You were changed by the pandemic and you have yet to talk about how deeply you have been affected." Your condition is called Post Traumatic Stress Disorder or a Post Traumatic Wound. There is help available, if you will risk talking about your emotions.

Some will; many will not and never will.

**Keywords:** gauntlet, trustworthy, schedule, freedom, new habits, help, risk

If yearning refers to what the new "normal" will be, what is your dream? Who will you be in the new "normal"?

# Z

## ZEN

*Out of the believer's heart shall flow rivers of living water.*
                                             John 7:38b, NRSV

ODD, IS IT NOT, that I should find in another faith tradition a word to describe my own Christian belief? Yet enlightenment is always a wonderful surprise and, in my tradition, evidence of God's present grace.

During this pandemic there have been tricky whirlpools of disinformation that have made attempts to apply mitigating practices difficult. The raging rapids of the news cycle have made presenting any coherent storyline impossible. And the steady drumbeats of Twitter drops raining down upon us have polluted the waters of truth.

Yet in spite of all the distractions, waters of revelation have washed over me. Sometimes that enlightenment has come in little drops that have slowly trickled down my cheeks. On occasions there have been veritable rivers of sweat. Every so often I have been caught in showers of unexpected blessings. Sometimes I find myself immersed in deep pools of caring, or maybe lulled by the rhythms of the steady rolling waves of compassion, or baptized by the steady watering of God's grace. It is all living water flowing from the heart of God to mine.

And my challenge is not to build a dam, or hide under an umbrella, or retreat somehow to the arid safety of fear, but to rather let the waters flow in me and through me until I am washed clean by God's grace.

So discuss how you experience the reality of my pandemic benediction.

*When you meet a person with a mask,*

> *may you see the eyes of God's beloved child;*
> *When you wash your hands,*
> *may you see the hands of God's beloved servant;*
> *and when you maintain that six feet of separation,*
> *may you bridge that space with a mutual blessing,*
> *one both given and received,*
> *wishing good health to the one you meet upon the trail,*
> *always looking for the gift that person brings to your life.*

**Keywords:** revelation, enlightenment, caring, compassion, grace, washed, blessing

The end of this alphabet is the beginning of the next. What kind of alphabet do you want to create with your life? What will be some of the words that you hope to include?

## FINAL THOUGHTS

EXAXCTLY WHAT ALL these words and emotions say about me, I am not sure. However, for the last one – enlightenment or wholeness – *Zen*, I have a pretty good idea and that makes me smile.

To explain what I mean I will share with you the first thing I wrote about my healing journey, a short article about an experience I had while I was in California. I mentioned in passing earlier. The title was "Staggering Meditation."

* * * * * * * *

In November 1992, Arnie K., Therese F., and Claude T. {three people connected with the Community of Mindful Living that was associated with the Vietnamese Buddhist monk Thich Nhat Hanh} came to share a Day of Mindfulness with a group of Vietnam veteran ministers. We could all sit, but walking meditation was difficult for a few of us. One man lost his legs in Vietnam; I injured a hip and knee during an incident and cannot walk slowly and deliberately without a cane. I mentioned to Therese that during the walking meditation, as I sat on the porch and watched, I had felt left out and separated from the group; half in jest, I said that what I needed was some form of "staggering meditation." She replied, "It's up to you to invent it."

That day I had left my wooden cane in a corner of my room at the retreat center. For years I have kept it hidden, having learned how to compensate for and disguise my painful problem with walking. That "stick" was a reminder of things I wanted to forget. I did not want to remember "Cripple Corner" in Danang, an intersection near a Vietnamese hospital where maimed Vietnamese soldiers, surrounded by canes, crutches, and makeshift wheelchairs, would gather to wait for an American convoy of large trucks to pass, hoping to be able to throw themselves, or be thrown by friends, under the huge tires so that their families could collect some monetary compensation from the U.S. government. Yet I could not forget. A few years ago, watching a parade in Wheeling, West Virginia, I knelt down beside my young son, and my hip went out and I could not get up, and I was one with the soldiers of years before, a "cripple" by the roadside. Shame, disgust, and despair welled up within me; my helplessness found a focus on that hated cane, and in my anger I would not use it.

When I returned to my room later that afternoon, I sat and thought about inventing "staggering meditation." I decided I would go for a walk, and rather than take my "stick" along as a necessary evil and out of anxiety over falling, I would "invite" my cane to be my helper. "Please come and be my companion," I said. So we set out to walk into the nearby city center. As we made our way along the sidewalks, I tried being aware not only of my breath but of my feet and the wooden cane in my hand. Many emotions and thoughts came and I greeted both the pleasant ones and the not-so-pleasant ones and invited them to join us in our walk. After a while, I became less aware of these emotions and thoughts and more aware of the ground on which I was walking, the beauty and gentle warmth of the evening, and the people around me. I even became thankful for the companion that supported me.

As I have continued my "staggering meditation" with my companion, I have tried to think deeply about this practice. For so many years, because of my anger, I deprived myself of the support that I needed to be fully mobile. When I did seek that support, I was motivated more by a fear of falling then anything else. I have come to awareness that my companion is a gift that helps connect me not only with the ground, but also with the many others who for a variety of reasons cannot walk easily, but also stagger. When I cam connected with these brother and sisters, I no longer feel separated or left out. Rather then a reminder of a terrible past, I have uncovered a deep root of present meaning in the "tree" that I hug in my hand.

* * * * * * * *

I wrote this first as a letter to the two leaders of that small group that came to our Conference meeting. That meeting had already profound affected me and this experience of reconciliation with my cane was icing on the rich cake of enlightenment that I had received, all of which combined I can only describe as a huge explosion going off in the mind and my soul.

In my experience, and I am sure it is true for many of us, I think of explosions as violent and destructive, blowing things up and apart. Certainly the results of the bombings that I occasionally had to evaluate in Vietnam supported that perception.

However, this violence, this explosion of enlightenment, was a creative, freeing force. It certainly challenged and destroyed the rather comfortable feelings I had developed about my cane for it is very easy to become accustomed to hatred, and despair, and helplessness, and to accept all those feelings as the "norm." But the relief I felt and the new freedom I enjoyed after I accepted my cane as a "gift" was so profound that I simply wanted to express my gratitude to them.

To my surprise they responded asking permission to publish what I had written as a short article in their magazine. In agreeing to that, I did wonder exactly what my Presbyterian colleagues would say about me having an article in a Buddhist magazine. Fortunately, none of them were subscribers to *The Mindfulness Bell*. And then I really did not care what they thought anyway. That was another gift arising out of this experience; I was freed from the belief that I had somehow to judge the value of my life by how I fulfilled others expectations.

That short article, only 615 words, became for me a guiding manifesto for life. That made me smile and still does. Later when the article was republished in two collections of writings (**A Joyful Path: Community Transformation and Peace** *[1994]* and **The Engaged Buddhist Reader** *[1996]*), the smile grew into a joyful grin.

I tell you this story, and I offer this video course of reflection, because I do not want any person, having come though this pandemic period of infection and riot, not to have an opportunity to address the storm of emotions that have been aroused and to find the joy of a smile. My hope is that doing so will save you, or your family, or others, from the hell of the delayed reactions that may come.

My faith tells me that the Creator has a hope for the beloved children. That dream of Shalom, of fullness of life, is summed up in the Book of Ecclesiastes (3:12,13):

*I know that there is nothing better for them [the children of God] than to be happy and enjoy themselves as long as they live; moreover, it is God's gift that all should eat and drink and take pleasure in all their toil.*

I wish you each "Shalom!"

## About the Author & Editor

ALAN CUTTER grew up in a pastor's family in Massachusetts, spending long summers at the family home in Southern Maine. Following in his Father's footsteps, he became a pastor, but only after serving on active duty in the US Navy for five years. This included a tour of duty in Vietnam. His pastorates were in Maine, New York, West Virginia and Minnesota; his last call was to be a church executive in South Louisiana following the trauma of hurricanes Katrina and Rita. When he was diagnosed with Agent Orange-related Parkinson's Disease in 2010, having previously been diagnosed with post-traumatic stress disorder, he retired. Alan has earned the following degrees a Bachelor's in English, (Syracuse, 68), a Master's in Library Science (Simmons, 70), a Master of Divinity (Bangor Seminary, 77) and a Doctor of Ministry (Pittsburgh, 96). The first two years of his military service were as an enlisted man going to various schools and studying North Vietnamese at the Defense Language Institute in Monterey, California. In late 1971, following his commissioning as an Ensign, he was sent directly to Vietnam, where he worked in and around Danang. While a member of the National Conference of Viet Nam Veteran Ministers, he edited the Vietnam Veterans of America Book of Prayers and Services. He has co-led numerous veterans' retreats on Trauma and Spirituality, spoken at the International Society of Traumatic Stress Studies, and been a consultant with the Canadian Armed Forces working with units deploying to Afghanistan. Currently he is president of the International Conference of War Veteran Ministers. He is married to Ann, who acts as his editor.

ANN CUTTER grew up in Maryland where her father was a civilian employee of the U.S. Army at Edgewood Arsenal. She attended the University of Delaware, earning Bachelors and Masters Degrees in American Studies. Alan and Ann have three children and four grandchildren.

Alan's novel *At the Altar of War* is available at Amazon and on Kindle.

His two books of meditations *(God's Story, My Story* and An *Alphabet of God, War and Hope)* are available on Amazon and Kindle.

*The Letter of Paul to the Beloved Warrior*, a previously unknown letter with a commentary is available in Amazon and Kindle.

A summary and explanation of the healing retreats Dr. Cutter led with others are contained in **Hope and Healing for Veterans: Resources for the Spiritual Journey**. This is available on Amazon.

Also available on Amazon is the transcription of conversations held in 1999 when the National Conference of Viet Nam Veteran Ministers met in Annual Conference. This book is titled *The Land of My Misfortunes: Vietnam, America, and the Book of Genesis*

Visit Alan's webpage: http://amazon.com/author/alancutter

Made in the USA
Coppell, TX
10 March 2022